Copyright

This document is geared towards providing exact and reliable information regarding the topic and issue covered. The publication is sold because the publisher is not required to render accounting officially permitted or otherwise qualified services. If advice is necessary, legal or professional, it should be ordered.

From a Declaration of Principles, which was accepted and approved equally by a Committee of the American Bar Association and a Committee of Publishers and Associations.

It is not legal to reproduce, duplicate, or transmit any part of this document electronically or in printed format. Recording this publication is strictly prohibited, and any storage of this document is prohibited unless the publisher gives written permission. All rights reserved.

The information provided herein is truthful and consistent in that any liability, in terms of inattention or otherwise, by any usage or abuse of any policies, processes, or directions contained within is the solitary and utter responsibility of the recipient reader. Under no circumstances will any legal obligation or blame be held against the publisher for any reparation, damages, or monetary loss due to the information herein, either directly or indirectly.

Respective authors own all copyrights not held by the publisher.

The information herein is offered solely for informational purposes and is universal. It is presented without a contract or any guaranteed assurance.

The trademarks used are without any consent, and the trademark publication is without permission or backing by the trademark owner. All trademarks and brands within this book are for clarifying purposes only and owned by the owners, not affiliated with this document.

I have recreated events, locales, and conversations for my memories of them. In some instances, I have changed the names of individuals and places to maintain their anonymity. I may have changed some identifying characteristics and details, such as physical properties, occupations, and areas of residence.

This book or parts thereof may not be reproduced in any form, stored in any retrieval system, or transmitted in any way by any means—electronic, mechanical, photocopy, recording, or otherwise—without prior written permission of the publisher, except as provided by United States of America copyright law. For permission requests, write to the publisher at "Attention: Permissions Coordinator" at the address below.

This memoir is a work of nonfiction. Names, characters, places, public or private institutions, corporations, towns, and incidents are a product of the author's life based on actual events. Some names and identifying details have been changed.

All rights reserved following the U.S. Copyright Act of 1976; the scanning, uploading, and electronic sharing of any part of this book without the publisher's permission is unlawful piracy and theft of the author's intellectual property. If you would like to use material from the book (other than for review purposes), prior written permission must be obtained by contacting the publisher at the following email address atlife@yahoo.com

BE YE HOLY

I appreciate your support of the author's rights.
1st edition: Be Ye Holy Survivor's Guide
© Copyright 2024 by Cheryl Remington – All rights reserved.

Contents

1. Dedication Page 1
2. Introduction 3
3. Caught Unaware 7
4. What God Hates 46
5. Games People Play 68
6. Trendsetters 98
7. Social Media 119
8. Trojan Horse 153
Endnotes 165

Chapter 1
Dedication Page

In 1995, I authored the first edition of "Be Ye Holy." At the time of writing, I didn't anticipate that the book would serve as an informative resource for the Christian community in addressing the pressing issues of that era.

My son JD has encouraged me to revisit and revive this work for years. However, I hesitated to confront the cultural challenges that have emerged over the past thirty years.

JD emphasized the importance of this book for contemporary readers. After several discussions, I revised and re-release "Be Ye Holy." This edition is titled the "Survivor's Guide" as it highlights the risks associated with occult practices and paganism, targeting those who wish to dedicate their lives to serving Adonai.

In heartfelt acknowledgment, I dedicate this book to my beloved son, JD, along with my grandchildren, Shaylynn and Kristopher, and to all the cherished extended family members and those who are yet to join us. After dedicating 55 years of my life to serving God, I have understood what truly brings Him honor and glory.

Use this survivor manual as a guideline to navigate the spiritual world.

JD, please pass along this critical information to my grandchildren. They must equip themselves to confront the challenges we face. Son, I sincerely appreciate your faith in this book and its significance in helping us navigate today's spiritual conflicts.

CHERYL REMINGTON

To my beloved grandson, Kris, reconnecting with you has brought immense joy. I am genuinely grateful that you have dedicated your life to the Lord. Please share this valuable information with everyone who seeks to honor and glorify God.

Chapter 2

Introduction

How can we discern truth, protect our souls, and walk a righteous path in a world drowning in distractions, deception, and disarray? "Be Ye Holy" is a clarion call to a higher way of living, blending compelling personal testimony, scriptural wisdom, and profound cultural critique to expose the spiritual battles around and within us. It is not just a book; it's a spiritual guide, a mirror for self-reflection, and a rallying cry for those seeking to reclaim their spiritual integrity.

The journey begins with an extraordinary encounter between the author and a high-ranking occultist, an event that unveils the dark forces infiltrating even the most sacred spaces. Through this harrowing experience, the reader is plunged into the reality of spiritual warfare and the cunning devices used to corrupt faith, sow confusion, and undermine God's truth. The author confronts these forces with raw honesty and unflinching courage, offering readers a blueprint to recognize and resist the enemy's tactics.

"Be Ye Holy" challenges cultural norms, dissecting the influence of fashion, entertainment, and technology in shaping our moral compass. From the historical evolution of hairstyles and clothing as expressions of rebellion or submission to the seductive grip of social media and the cell phone as the Trojan Horse of the modern age, the book exposes how society's trends subtly erode spiritual values. It asks readers to reconsider what they invite into their homes and hearts, shedding light on the spiritual implications of seemingly innocent choices.

Historical insights: the book examines movements that sought to challenge societal and gender norms, revealing their roots in deeper spiritual battles. Whether it's the feminist pioneers who inadvertently invited spiritual rebellion or the entertainment industry's role in turning television into a modern-day altar of worship, "Be Ye Holy" peels back the layers to show how history repeats itself in more cunning and disguised forms. This book will open your eyes to the spiritual battles that have shaped our world and equip you to recognize and resist those same battles in your own life.

However, this book doesn't just point out the problems; it equips readers with practical solutions. Anchored in scripture, it explores humility, forgiveness, and faith themes. It calls readers to embrace repentance's power and find strength in obedience to God's Word. Through practical advice and spiritual principles, the author offers tools to cultivate discernment, set healthy boundaries, and stand firm in a world of compromise. This book will empower you to navigate the challenges of modern life with confidence and faith.

In its most potent moments, "Be Ye Holy" challenges the reader to consider the deeper meaning of holiness: not just a state of moral uprightness but a lifestyle of radical love, unwavering truth, and unshakable faith. It explores what it means to be set apart in a culture that celebrates conformity and chaos, urging believers to live as beacons of light in dark times.

This book is for anyone who has ever questioned the erosion of faith in modern society, has felt the tension between worldly pressures and spiritual convictions, and longs for a deeper relationship with God.

Whether confronting pride, seeking clarity in your faith, or simply yearning for a fresh start, "Be Ye Holy" will inspire and challenge you to rise above the noise and distractions of this age and walk boldly in the holiness you were called to.

"Be Ye Holy" is more than a title—it is a charge, a mission, and a reminder that amidst the chaos of the modern world, God's call remains clear: Be Ye Holy, for I Am Holy.

This gripping and transformative book will open your eyes, strengthen your spirit, and prepare you to navigate today's spiritual battles with courage, wisdom, and grace. Will you answer the call?

This book is based on historical documented facts and expounds on scriptures.

Be Ye Holy Leviticus 20:6-8 NLT: "I will also turn against those who commit spiritual prostitution by putting their trust in mediums or in those who consult the spirits of the dead. I will cut them off from the community. So set yourselves apart to be holy, for I am the LORD your God. Keep all my decrees by putting them into practice, for I am the LORD who makes you holy.

Chapter 3
Caught Unaware

For the sake of this story, I will call the men Tom and Jerry.

It was on a Sunday night in 1994 when a high-ranking Satanist visited my Church. He was invited by his close friend Jerry, whom I had met at another local assembly during a special event.

After service, Tom and Jerry went next door to the Church to eat pizza. I went into my office to regain my composure after an exhausting day. All this happened back when I believed the Sabbath was Sunday. The revelation of that truth came during my research.

I was in the office briefly when my assistant came in and told me that both gentlemen wanted me to join them next door. I told her that I wasn't interested. She said you might want to go; they seemed determined to meet with you.

With a sense of reluctance, I made my way next door. As I sat at the table, a sudden revelation struck me. Without a moment's hesitation, I fixed my gaze on Tom and demanded to know what he was doing in my Church.

Jerry's reaction was shock and disbelief at the directness of my approach. It was clear that he was unaware of Tom's true intentions.

Immediately, I asked Tom, "Are you going to tell your friend what we are talking about, or am I?" Tom looked at Jerry and said, "I am involved in some things at work."

That was too vague for me. So, I opened the can of worms and asked him why he would practice the occult.

Tom could tell that I knew what he was involved in, so he started telling me how he worked for the city of Dallas in the justice department and how they would deal with criminals. In some cases, it was for human sacrifices.

I asked him why he was at my Church. He said he had heard that I was honest.

What came out of his mouth will forever be etched in my memory. He said let me tell you why I don't serve your God. You Christians are stupid. You don't know we have moved our devices into your churches and homes. If your God was so great, why hasn't he exposed this to you?

I stopped him immediately and said, "Wait, right there. I take responsibility for my actions. Don't you ever put that on God? I am the one who is deaf and dumb, but if you are talking about crystals, potpourri, candles, unicorns, etc., I have only mentioned a few things because, at that point, I hadn't done very much research. In recent years, I have learned about the New Age and New World order by reading a book by Texe Marrs.

Tom then looked at me and said, "You must be stopped; you know too much." I responded, "If you think I know a lot now, just wait."

The next day, Stacey and I took our backpacks to the University of Texas at Arlington, and that day started our journey of investigation. Determined to discover what had happened to the Christian faith, I put my head on the desk with my Bible and asked God to lead me.

In the last 35 years, I have discovered everything happening in religion. What I share in my books is documented.

When reading this series, please don't take me for my word. Do your research.

The debate about the wearing of jewelry is ongoing and engaging. On one side, some declare that if the Lord had not wanted us to wear gold and silver, He would not have created it.

Some point out that God did not require the people to remove their jewelry; it was Aaron.

It's important to note that Aaron, a figure of authority, made the idol or golden calf with the ornaments. This should serve as a cautionary tale, reminding us to be mindful of the potential misuse of jewelry.

Are there deeper meanings behind jewelry, and how is it connected to the occult?

What you wear summons demon powers. These wicked entities know that we are ignorant of these powerful symbols.

Rest assured. I have provided the scriptures in this book so that you don't have to find a Bible and look them up. I also use the NLT, an easier-to-understand translation than the King James Version.

Understanding the enemy's cunning devices is crucial to gaining power over him. This knowledge empowers us and gives us control in our spiritual journey.

Understanding the enemy's cunning devices is not just a suggestion; it's a necessity.

This knowledge enlightens us with the necessary tools to navigate our spiritual path.

Exodus 32:1 NLT: *When the people saw how long it was taking Moses to come back down the mountain, they gathered around Aaron. "Come on," they said, "make us some gods* who can lead us. We don't know what happened to this fellow Moses, who brought us here from the land of Egypt."

Exodus 32:2 NLT: *So Aaron said, "Take the gold rings from the ears of your wives and sons and daughters, and bring them to me."*

Exodus 32:3 NLT: *All the people took the gold rings from their ears and brought them to Aaron.*

Exodus 32:4 NLT: *Then Aaron took the gold, melted it down, and molded it into the shape of a calf. When the people saw it, they exclaimed, "O Israel, these are the gods who brought you out of the land of Egypt!"*

Exodus 32:5 NLT: *Aaron saw how excited the people were, so he built an altar in front of the calf. Then he announced, "Tomorrow will be a festival to the LORD!"*

Exodus 32:6 NLT: *The people got up early the next morning to sacrifice burnt offerings and peace offerings.* <u>*After this, they celebrated with feasting and drinking, and they indulged in pagan revelry.*</u>

Exodus 32:7 NLT: *The LORD told Moses, "Quick! Go down the mountain! Your people whom you brought from the land of Egypt have corrupted themselves.*

Exodus 32:8 NLT: *How quickly they have turned away from the way I commanded them to live! They have melted down gold and made a calf, and they have bowed down and sacrificed to it. They are saying, 'These are your gods, O Israel, who brought you out of the land of Egypt.'"*

Exodus 32:9 NLT: <u>*Then the LORD said, "I have seen how stubborn and rebellious these people are.*</u>

Exodus 32:10 NLT: <u>*Now leave me alone so my fierce anger can blaze against them, and I will destroy them. Then I will make you, Moses, into a great nation."*</u>

Exodus 32:11 NLT: <u>But Moses tried to pacify the LORD his God. "O LORD!" he said. "Why are you so angry with your own people whom you brought from the land of Egypt with such great power and such a strong hand?</u>

Exodus 32:12 NLT: <u>Why let the Egyptians say, 'Their God rescued them with the evil intention of slaughtering them in the mountains and wiping them from the face of the earth'? Turn away from your fierce anger. Change your mind about this terrible disaster you have threatened against your people!</u>

Exodus 32:13 NLT: <u>Remember your servants Abraham, Isaac, and Jacob. You bound yourself with an oath to them, saying, 'I will make your descendants as numerous as the stars of heaven. And I will give them all of this land that I have promised to your descendants, and they will possess it forever.'"</u>

Exodus 32:14 NLT: <u>The LORD changed his mind about the terrible disaster he had threatened to bring on his people.</u>

The Lord's request is in the next chapter. Notice that this is the first time Adonai meets with Moses in the tent of meeting. Pay close attention to that.

Exodus 33:4 NLT: **<u>When the people heard these stern words, they went into mourning and stopped wearing their jewelry and fine clothes.</u>**

Exodus 33:5 NLT: **<u>For the LORD had told Moses to tell them, "You are a stubborn and rebellious people. If I were to travel with you for even a moment, I would destroy you. Remove your jewelry and fine clothes while I decide what to do with you."</u>**

Exodus 33:6 NLT: **<u>So, when they left Mount Sinai, the Israelites wore no more jewelry or fine clothes.</u>**

Exodus 33:7 NLT: <u>It was Moses' practice to take the Tent of Meeting and set it up some distance from the camp. Everyone who wanted to make a request of the LORD would go to the Tent of Meeting outside the camp.</u>

Exodus 33:8 NLT: <u>Whenever Moses went out to the Tent of Meeting, all the people would get up and stand in the entrances of their own tents. They would all watch Moses until he disappeared inside.</u>

Exodus 33:9 NLT: <u>As he went into the tent, the pillar of cloud would come down and hover at its entrance while the LORD spoke with Moses.</u>

Exodus 33:10 NLT: <u>When the people saw the cloud standing at the tent's entrance, they would bow down in front of their tents.</u>

Exodus 33:11 NLT: <u>Inside the Tent of Meeting, the LORD would speak to Moses face to face, as one speaks to a friend. Afterward Moses would return to the camp, but the young man who assisted him, Joshua son of Nun, would remain behind in the Tent of Meeting.</u>

In the 33rd chapter of Exodus, the children of Israel were told to remove their ornaments forever. Before that period, they did wear jewelry. When they took the ornaments off, God met with them. Compare the difference between serving the Almighty God and pagan worship, which was associated with the representation of the ornaments.

Exodus 35:20 NLT: <u>So the whole community of Israel left Moses and returned to their tents.</u>

Exodus 35:21 NLT: <u>All whose hearts were stirred and whose spirits were moved came and brought their sacred offerings to the LORD. They brought all the materials needed for the Tabernacle, for the performance of its rituals, and for the sacred garments.</u>

Exodus 35:22 NLT: <u>Both men and women came, all whose hearts were willing. They brought to the LORD their offerings of gold--brooches, earrings, rings from their fingers, and necklaces. They presented gold objects of every kind as a special offering to the LORD.</u>

Exodus 35:23 NLT: <u>All those who owned the following items willingly brought them: blue, purple, and scarlet thread; fine linen and goat hair for cloth; and tanned ram skins and fine goatskin leather.</u>

Exodus 35:24 NLT: <u>And all who had silver and bronze objects gave them as a sacred offering to the LORD. And those who had acacia wood brought it for use in the project.</u>

Exodus 35:25 NLT: <u>All the women who were skilled in sewing and spinning prepared blue, purple, and scarlet thread, and fine linen cloth.</u>

Exodus 35:26 NLT: <u>All the women who were willing used their skills to spin the goat hair into yarn.</u>

Exodus 35:27 NLT: <u>The leaders brought onyx stones and the special gemstones to be set in the ephod and the priest's chestpiece.</u>

Exodus 35:28 NLT: <u>They also brought spices and olive oil for the light, the anointing oil, and the fragrant incense.</u>

Exodus 35:29 NLT: <u>So the people of Israel--every man and woman who was eager to help in the work the LORD had given them through Moses--brought their gifts and gave them freely to the LORD.</u>

Exodus 35:20-29 relates that they brought their jewels into the Tabernacle as an offering. The gold was to be used to make the items of service unto the Lord.

According to history, the precious minerals and stones were used to worship pagan deities. The following excerpts illustrate.

GODS, PAGAN: The false gods and idols were worshiped by people during Bible times -- especially the false gods of Egypt, Mesopotamia (Assyria and Babylon), Canaan, Greece, and Rome. Religion has always played an essential part in civilization; in the ancient world, it was a powerful force. The pagan civilizations of Bible times worshiped many gods. There were male and female deities, high and low gods, assemblies of gods, priests and priestesses, temples, and sacrifices. All the forces of nature that could not be controlled or understood were considered supernatural powers to be worshiped and feared.

Our knowledge of the pagan gods of the ancient world comes from the religious literature, idols, and other objects discovered by archaeologists. We have also learned from the meanings of names found in the literature from this period. People in Bible times were often named with sentences and phrases; sometimes, they used the name of their favorite god in the compound name. Thus, names very often reflected popular religion. Most of the ancient world was polytheistic; they worshiped more than one god.

The people worshiped these gods in the form of representative idols. This practice is called idolatry. The nation of Israel, however, was forbidden to make graven images of the one true and living God whom they worshiped Exodus 20:3-6; Deuteronomy 5:7-10. The pagan nations made statues or images representing the powers they worshiped. Most of these idols were in the form of animals or men. But sometimes, these idols represented celestial powers like the sun, moon, and stars, forces of nature like the sea and the rain, or life forces like death and truth. [1]

Exodus 35:20 NLT: So the whole community of Israel left Moses and returned to their tents.

Exodus 35:21 NLT: All whose hearts were stirred and whose spirits were moved came and brought their sacred offerings to the LORD. They brought all the materials needed for the Tabernacle, for the performance of its rituals, and for the sacred garments.

Exodus 35:22 NLT; Both men and women came, all whose hearts were willing. They brought to the LORD their offerings of gold--brooches, earrings, rings from their fingers, and necklaces. They presented gold objects of every kind as a special offering to the LORD.

Exodus 35:23 NLT: All those who owned the following items willingly brought them: blue, purple, and scarlet thread; fine linen and goat hair for cloth; and tanned ram skins and fine goatskin leather.

Exodus 35:24 NLT: And all who had silver and bronze objects gave them as a sacred offering to the LORD. And those who had acacia wood brought it for use in the project.

In this chapter, I will address these various pieces of jewelry. You will learn their hidden meaning and purpose.

Deuteronomy 7:25 NLT: <u>**"You must burn their idols in fire, and you must not covet the silver or gold that covers them. You must not take it or it will become a trap to you, for it is detestable to the LORD your God.**</u>

Deuteronomy 7:26 NLT: <u>**Do not bring any detestable objects into your home, for then you will be destroyed, just like them. You must utterly detest such things, for they are set apart for destruction.**</u>

"In time, an elaborate system of beliefs about such natural forces was developed into mythology. Each civilization and culture had its mythological structure, which was often quite similar. The names of the gods may have been different, but their functions and actions were often the same." [2]

"According to the Old Testament, God was a jealous God who permitted no rivals: 'You shall have no other gods before Me' Exodus 20:3; Deuteronomy 5:7. God's Will is all-powerful, and man must submit to it. He reveals Himself when He pleases and to whom He pleases, demanding that man obey His revelation. Nevertheless, the Hebrew people sometimes gave in to temptation and worshiped these pagan gods from the surrounding cultures." [3]

Exodus 20:1 NLT: <u>Then God gave the people all these instructions:</u>

Exodus 20:2 NLT: <u>"I am the LORD your God, who rescued you from the land of Egypt, the place of your slavery.</u>

Exodus 20:3 NLT: <u>"You must not have any other god but me.</u>

Exodus 20:4 NLT: <u>"You must not make for yourself an idol of any kind or an image of anything in the heavens or on the Earth or in the sea.</u>

Exodus 20:5 NLT: <u>You must not bow down to them or worship them, for I, the LORD your God, am a jealous God who will not tolerate your affection for any other gods. I lay the sins of the parents upon their children; the entire family is affected--even children in the third and fourth generations of those who reject me.</u>

Exodus 20:6 NLT: <u>But I lavish unfailing love for a thousand generations on those who love me and obey my commands.</u>

Deuteronomy 5:6 NLT: <u>"I am the LORD your God, who rescued you from the land of Egypt, the place of your slavery.</u>

Deuteronomy 5:7 NLT: <u>"You must not have any other god but me.</u>

Deuteronomy 5:8 NLT: <u>"You must not make for yourself an idol of any kind, or an image of anything in the heavens or on the Earth or in the sea.</u>

Deuteronomy 5:9 NLT: <u>***You must not bow down to them or worship them, for I, the LORD your God, am a jealous God who will not tolerate your affection for any other gods. I lay the sins of the parents upon their children; the entire family is affected--even children in the third and fourth generations of those who reject me.***</u>

Deuteronomy 5:10 NLT: <u>***But I lavish unfailing love for a thousand generations on those who love me and obey my commands.***</u>

"The many pagan gods that served as a temptation to the Hebrew people may be conveniently grouped into four distinct types: the false gods of (1) Mesopotamia (Assyria and Babylon), (2) Egypt, (3) Canaan, and (4) Greece and Rome." [4]

THE PAGAN GODS OF MESOPOTAMIA:
"As Mesopotamian religion developed, each god had his stars, which became popular with the development of ASTROLOGY. Many of the astrological texts and charts of the ancient Babylonians read like modern horoscopes." [5]

THE PAGAN GODS OF EGYPT: The gods of Egypt were a constant threat to the Israelites, both during their years in bondage and afterward. Their deliverance from Egypt was described by the Bible as a great spiritual victory, with the sovereign Lord of Israel defeating the gods of the Egyptians Exodus 18:11; 2 Samuel 7:23. Egyptian religion reflected the same pagan ideas that were popular in the ancient world but with different figures. Horus was the god of Egypt's western delta, a human figure with a falcon's head. Hathor, the corresponding goddess, had a cow's body and a woman's head. The god, Set, had a man's body and an animal's head. Anubis had a man's body and the head of an ibis. Besides gods that were composite of animal and human forms, some Egyptian gods were portrayed as entirely human. [6]

Exodus 18:10 NLT: "Praise the LORD," Jethro said, "for he has rescued you from the Egyptians and from Pharaoh. Yes, he has rescued Israel from the powerful hand of Egypt!

Exodus 18:11 NLT: <u>*I know now that the LORD is greater than all other gods, because he rescued his people from the oppression of the proud Egyptians."*</u>

2 Samuel 7:22 NLT: <u>*"How great you are, O Sovereign LORD! There is no one like you. We have never even heard of another God like you!*</u>

2 Samuel 7:23 NLT: *What other nation on Earth is like your people Israel? What other nation, O God, have you redeemed from slavery to be your own people? You made a great name for yourself when you redeemed your people from Egypt. You performed awesome miracles and drove out the nations and gods that stood in their way.*

2 Samuel 7:24 NLT: <u>*You made Israel your very own people forever, and you, O LORD, became their God.*</u>

"In ancient Egyptian religion, Osiris was the god of the lower world and judge of the dead. He was the brother and husband of Isis and father (or brother) of Horus. Osiris is killed by Set, who is jealous of his power. Isis, the ancient Egyptian goddess of fertility, persuaded the gods to bring back Osiris, her dead husband. The myth is, therefore, an ancient vegetation cycle." [7]

"The Egyptians portrayed many of their gods with animal images. But they also had their cosmic deities." [8]

"The Egyptians also worshiped the sun, moon, and stars. Ra (also Re), the sun god, was the supreme deity of the ancient Egyptians." [9]

"The Egyptians had many other pagan gods." [10]

"The worship of all the gods also involved magic and superstition. The purpose of these gods was to explain the cycle and forces of life and to ensure stability and fertility." [11]

"Baal and related deities are also portrayed as a mating bull, symbolizing fertility. Unsurprisingly, while Moses was on Mount Sinai, receiving the Ten Commandments from the Lord, the disobedient Israelites fashioned a golden calf to worship Exodus 32." 12

"During the history of the Israelites, a rivalry developed between Baalism and the true worship of the Lord Jeremiah 23:27. Perhaps the best example of this rivalry was the conflict between Elijah and the prophets of Baal on Mount Carmel 1 Kings 18. Elijah's challenge to them to bring down fire from heaven was appropriate because the Canaanites believed that Baal could shoot lightning flashes from the sky. Elijah's mocking of Baal struck at the heart of their claims; he knew that Baal was powerless, that the prophets of Baal had misled the people, and that only the Lord God of Israel was alive and able to answer. In the struggle to the death between true and false religion, Elijah knew that Baalism and its prophets had to be destroyed." 13

Jeremiah 23:25 NLT: <u>"I have heard these prophets say, 'Listen to the dream I had from God last night.' And then they proceed to tell lies in my name.</u>

Jeremiah 23:26 NLT: <u>How long will this go on? If they are prophets, they are prophets of deceit, inventing everything they say.</u>

Jeremiah 23:27 NLT: <u>By telling these false dreams, they are trying to get my people to forget me, just as their ancestors did by worshiping the idols of Baal.</u>

"Like the myths of many pagan religions, Canaanite stories claim Baal came to prominence by defeating other gods." 14

"...the Assyro-Babylonian goddess Ishtar. Anat was the patroness of sex and passion; lewd figurines of this nude goddess have been discovered at various archaeological sites in Palestine." 15

In the Old and New Testaments, the people of God were surrounded by pagan gods. The apostle Paul declared to the philosophers of Athens, 'I perceive that in all things you are very religious' Acts 17:22. In the city of Athens, idols of pagan gods stood on every street corner. The Athenians, perhaps fearing that they had slighted some deity, had even erected an altar 'to the unknown god' Acts 17:23. [16]

The One whom you worship without knowing,' said Paul, 'Him I proclaim to you: God, who made the world and everything in it, since He is Lord of heaven and Earth, does not dwell in temples made with hands' Acts 17:23-24.16 [17]

Acts 17:22 NLT: <u>So Paul, standing before the council, addressed them as follows: "Men of Athens, I notice that you are very religious in every way,</u>

Acts 17:23 NLT: <u>for as I was walking along I saw your many shrines. And one of your altars had this inscription on it: 'To an Unknown God.' This God, whom you worship without knowing, is the one I'm telling you about.</u>

Acts 17:24 NLT: <u>"He is the God who made the world and everything in it. Since he is Lord of heaven and Earth, he doesn't live in man-made temples,</u>

AMULET: "A word first used to designate objects having a magical effect in warding off or driving away evils - the evil eye, illness, demons, etc. - and thus practically equivalent to TALISMAN. By degrees, it came to be employed for objects worn about the person." [18]

"In the Old Testament, objects of the kind are mentioned among the ornaments worn by women Isaiah 3:16-26) and by animals (Judges 8:21); the bells on the border of the high priest's robe had no other primary significance (compare 'the bells of the horses,' Zachariah 14:20). Later Judaism surrounded the individual with intangible spirits, but provided numerous means of protection against the evil they might affect - the presence of angels, pronouncing the name of God, amulets containing the Holy Name, and fragments of Scripture person (the 'phylacteries' of Matthew 23:5) or fastened to the door posts of the houses. The extraordinary power over demons attributed to Solomon may also be mentioned; formulas of exorcism were referred to him, and the possessed were supposed to be healed, on the invocation of his name, by his prescribed methods.

The demonological conceptions of Judaism and the magic of the East strongly influenced the Greco-Roman world. However, Christianity initially rejected these superstitious observances and protested against every accusation of the use of magic arts. Then, with the entrance of the pagan multitudes, with their material ideas of religion and their need for an external realization of the supernatural, a change occurred. [19]

"...magical formulas began to be used again; inscribed with characters often unintelligible, mysterious objects were placed upon the bodies of newborn infants and the sick." [20]

'The teachers of the Church branded all this as actual apostasy from the faith, and the Christian civil government punished severely the use of amulets in sickness." [21]

"The demons, who had been supposed to have special care of races or individuals, now became ANGELS, and protection was afforded by their names inscribed on amulets. In like manner, the name of God was used. Even some clergy provided such amulets, though the Church forbade them to do so and excommunicated those who wore them (Synod of Laodicea; Synod of Agde, 544). The cross (See Cross and Its Uses as a Symbol, 3) was especially prominent among these protecting objects. Women and children commonly wore verses from the Gospels for this purpose." [22]

The whole range of sacred things was brought into service.

"Since the Church was unable entirely and all at once to drive out every vestige of heathen superstition, it did the next best thing when it took into consideration the needs of popular, unspiritual devotion, and gradually, by the conversion of the old means, forced into the background or effaced their non - Christian elements." [23]

"DRESS AND ORNAMENT, HEBREW"

CHARMS: "A jewel was at the same time an amulet. According to the ancient Oriental view, metals and precious stones belonged to certain gods of the mineral world and possessed, therefore, a mysterious magic power. Aside from this, any trinket that diverts attention from the wearer to itself still protects against the evil eye. For this reason, everyone in the Orient wears an abundance of jewelry. Traces of this superstition are found in the Old Testament. In Isaiah 3:20, a piece of woman's jewelry is designated as an amulet (compare Genesis 35: 4), and it is evident that the ornaments on the camels of the Midianites were charms (Judges 8:21). In design and execution, the various articles of jewelry resemble Babylonian and Egyptian models." [24]

"THE ART OF BEDOUIN JEWELRY"
CHARMS: "As jewelry components, charms (ahjibah, singular hijab) have a long history. Charm cases, worn as pendants, were common in Persia in the second and third centuries A.D. and had religious and superstitious significance. They enjoyed renewed popularity in Persia in the late twelfth and thirteenth centuries." [25]

"THE ENCYCLOPEDIA OF WITCHES AND WITCHCRAFT"
TALISMANS: "Objects that possess magical or supernatural power and transmit them to the owner. Talismans often are confused with AMULETS, objects that passively protect their wearers from evil and harm. Talismans usually perform a single function and enable powerful transformations. The magic wand of a sorcerer or fairy, King Arthur's sword Excalibur, seven-league boots, and Mercury's helmet of invisibility are all talismans.

A talisman can be any object, but according to magic, it can be endowed with supernatural power only by the forces of nature, by God or the gods, or by being made in a ritualistic way. Precious stones, for example, have always been considered talismans, each having its own magical or curative powers endowed by nature.

Talismans are found in all cultures and throughout history. They were common in ancient Egypt and Babylonia, where they were used to try to alter the forces of nature. In the Middle Ages, holy objects were valued as talismans for their ability to cure illness. [26]

AMULETS:
"Man's desire to protect himself against bad luck, illness, and evil is as old as man himself. From the days of the earliest cave dwellers, the amulet, an object imbued with mysterious and magical properties, has offered protection. Amulets are universal. The objects may

come and go in fashion, but their purpose endures, no matter how 'civilized' a society may be.

Amulets are answers to age-old needs: to be healthy, to be virile and fertile, to be robust and successful, to have good fortune. To ancient man, these needs were controlled by the invisible forces of good and evil. PRAYERS, SACRIFICES, and offerings induced the good spirits to grant blessings; amulets prevented the evil spirits from taking them away. Originally, amulets were natural objects whose unusual shapes or colors attracted attention. The magical properties of such objects were presumed to be inherent. As civilization advanced, amulets became more diverse. They were fashioned into animal shapes, symbols, RINGS, seals, and plaques and were imbued with magical power with inscriptions or spells.

Amulet comes from the Latin word amuletum or the Old Latin term amoletum, which means "means of defense." The Roman naturalist Pliny defined three basic types of amulets: those offering protection against trouble and adversity, medical or prophylactic treatment, and substances used in medicine. Many subdivisions are within these three general categories, for no one amulet is broadly multipurpose. Amulets with inscriptions are also called CHARMS. An amulet is typically worn on the body - usually hung around the neck - but some amulets guard tombs, homes, and buildings.

The ancient Egyptians, Assyrians, Babylonians, Arabs, and Hebrews placed great importance on amulets. The Egyptians used them everywhere. The frog protected fertility; ANKHS were linked to everlasting life and generation; the udjat, or eye, was for good health, comfort, and protection against evil; the scarab beetle was for resurrection after death and protection against evil magic." [27]

"The Assyrians and Babylonians used cylinder seals embedded with semiprecious and precious stones, each with unique magical powers. Various animal shapes served as amulets; for example, the ram for virility and the bull for virility and strength. The Arabs gathered dust from tombs and carried it in little sacks as protection against evil." [28]

"Hebrews wore crescent moons to ward off the EVIL EYE and attached BELLS to their clothing to ward off evil spirits." [29]

"In all cultures, holy books such as the Koran, Torah, and Bible are considered to have protective powers. Bits of parchment with scripture quotes, carried in leather pouches or silver boxes, are amulets in various religions. Ancient pagans wore figurines of the gods as amulets. This custom was absorbed into the Catholic Church.

In neo-Pagan Witchcraft, the most powerful amulet is the silver pentacle, the religious symbol of the Craft. Silver, in general, is held to have amuletic properties and is used in jewelry along with various crystals and gems. [30]

"ENCYCLOPEDIA BRITANNICA, INC. "1970

JEWELRY: "The history of wearing jewels is as old as the history of mankind. Apart from their decorative value, ornaments have been worn as charms and amulets from ancient times. In Arabia, Persia, and China, green stones used to be placed in the mouths of the dead because they were supposed to contain life-giving substances. This old conception about green stones persists, though in a modified form. Jade, even today, is widely believed, in Persia and India, to have the power to protect the wearer from heart diseases and the turquoise to ward off approaching danger. From time to time, various precious stones have been associated with different stars and worn to receive special protection from them. Even metals have not escaped such an interpretation. 'Those who wear gold ornaments live a long time in the abodes of the gods' was a belief not confined to India. From the very early period, Egyptians and Sumerians also decorated themselves with GOLD and SILVER ornaments because they thought these metals had magical powers. An investigation of the symbolism of ornaments, especially, reveals the belief in their magico - religious value - a belief inherent in a vestigial form in, for example, the wearing of birthstones." [31]

"The wearing of important jewelry has been associated with solemn occasions in the community's life." [32]

"Whether worn for personal enjoyment, to display power or wealth, for protection against harm, or as part of ceremonial dress, it is in the association with the individual wearer that the jewel has its primary importance." [33]

"Real jewelry, when not worn for want of occasion, loses much of the awe it was intended to inspire: the talismanic stone from which the aura of belief has been dissipated, the chieftain's great brooch, chain or bracelets whose original intention was to transform the ordinary man into the lawgiver, the ruler or the god, lose something by deprivation of the context in which they originally confronted the community. Jewels become lifeless artifacts when studied apart from it." [34]

In every definition shown here from research, it is a common fact that amulets, charms, talismans, and jewelry have all represented magical, mystical, and occultic beliefs. What God are we serving if we are wearing such? The New Age teaches that Jesus Christ does not exist—we are gods. Therefore, by wearing ornaments, we are adorning ourselves as actual deities.

Our research revealed that no precious minerals or stones are found naturally in the land of Israel. It is a pure and holy land, a true example of how God wants His people to live. God knew that men's hearts would be easily affected by the conduct of the others around them. Suppose God had intended His people to be wealthy in natural minerals after forty years of wandering. In that case, He could have led them to a surrounding country, such as Africa, which is rich in natural resources. Instead, He led them to a place where there were none. God knew that paganistic ideas would infiltrate His people and wanted a righteous nation. He wanted them to learn the true meaning of freedom and not bondage.

"THE NEW ENCYCLOPEDIA BRITANNICA" 1992

ISRAEL: Resources. Mineral Resources. "Mineral resources include potash, bromine, and magnesium, the last two of which are obtained from the waters of the Dead Sea; copper ore, which is located in the `Arava Valley; phosphates and small amounts of gypsum in the Negev; and some marble in Galilee. There are oil deposits in the northern

Negev and south of Tel Aviv, as well as natural gas deposits in the northern Negev and northeast of Beersheba. Limited exploration of oil began in the 1950's." [35]

Trade. "Imports are mainly raw materials, including rough diamonds and capital goods. Exports include light industrial products, textiles, polished diamonds, fertilizer and chemical products, and agricultural produce (mainly citrus fruits)." [36]

Let's find out what other reference books say about the symbolism behind the jewels.

"DICTIONARY OF SYMBOLS"
PRECIOUS AND SEMIPRECIOUS STONES: "By their beauty, these stones have more than ornamental function: with their colors and other characteristics, they also influence the imagination. We are concerned here with relatively hard minerals that can be cut, as well as (by common usage) organic materials like CORAL and AMBER, which are of importance primarily as talismans and amulets but can also function symbolically. Polished and shiny, gems can also serve as MIRRORS. JADE, which occurs in countless varieties, is for the Chinese a symbol of diversity and the infinite; its durability was believed to conserve bodies after burial. These STONES in general, since they reveal their beauty only when they are cut and polished, can symbolize humanity itself, in its need for refinement. On the other hand, CRYSTALS occurring gem-like in nature symbolize perfect virtue." [37]

"Reflecting gems, especially crystals, were often used as aids to meditation and believed to have healing properties. Ancient books of stone lore, called "lithic," treat the magic correspondences between planets, personality types, and "power stones," which are supposed to have a great variety of effects. In symbology, along with rock–crystal, DIAMONDS, AMETHYSTS, RUBIES, jade, TURQUOISES, SAPPHIRES, and EMERALDS are especially important." [38]

"The individual planets with their unique powers are also symbolized by gems, from which pieces of jewelry were made to be worn by persons feeling themselves particularly linked to the heavenly body in question.

The most common pairings are as follows: Thus SUN–diamond, rock–crystal, bright-colored varieties of zircon, tourmaline, and cairngorm; the MOON–pearls, adularia, agate; MARS–ruby, garnet, coral, carnelian; MERCURY–beryl, tiger–eye, topaz, agate, amber, zircon; JUPITER–emerald, GREEN turquoise, jade, serpentine, malachite; VENUS–lapis lazuli, sapphire, aquamarine; SATURN–amethyst, dark varieties of onyx and sapphire." [39]

GEMS:

Agate: "...It was believed to possess magical powers - warding off storms, keeping RIVERS from overflowing their banks, bringing luck against an opponent, exerting aphrodisiac powers over women." [40]

Amethyst: "...Was considered a symbol of modesty, peace of mind, and piety, but also associated with powers of mental healing. In ancient times, it was thought to protect against drunkenness." [41]

Diamonds: (Diamonds will be covered under the title of rings)

Emerald: "The emerald brings reason, wisdom, and dexterity...." [42] Ancient volumes devoted to STONE lore attributed to the emerald the power to dispel STORMS and liberate slaves." [43]

Jade: "Translucent, emerald-green pieces were most prized and felt to symbolize purity, wisdom, and courage. As early as 3000 B.C., ritual instruments and jewelry were made from this jade; around 1500 B. C., carved FISH, BIRDS, and DRAGONS. The lasting beauty of these objects led to the belief that jade had within it the quality of immortality. Jade amulets were placed on the dead's lips, faces, or chests and buried with them." [44]

Pearl: "...It symbolized for the Gnostics of late antiquity hidden knowledge and esoteric wisdom, and for Christians the teachings of Jesus, which were inaccessible to nonbelievers." [45]

"...A string of pearls is a frequent analogy for the multitude of God's powers." [46]

Rubies and Garnets: "Ancient books of "stone" lore refer to their power to protect against shipwrecks. The ruby came to symbolize vitality, royalty, and passionate love. In the Book of Revelation, God's glory is likened to diamonds and rubies." [47]

Turquoise: "It was thought to protect rulers from evil influences. In ancient Mexico, turquoise (in Aztec, xihuitl) was one of the most admired gemstones; only JADE was more valued. Turquoise mosaics adorned the DIADEM of the KINGS and their ornamental shields. The FIRE god was called "Lord of the Turquoise" (Xiuhtecutli) -- the sky-blue turquoise symbolizing the unity of heavenly (i.e., solar) and earthly FIRE. He was adorned with the "turquoise serpent" (Xiuhcoatl), which also constituted his "alter ego"; the Aztec king was considered to be his earthly counterpart." [48]

CHAIN: "Originally a symbol of imprisonment and slavery, or defeat...In many contexts, BROKEN chains symbolize the overcoming of servitude. In FREEMASONRY symbolism, the "fraternal chain" is the bond between brother Masons, expressed at the conclusion of the WORK of the lodge by the joining of hands in a CIRCLE." [49]

BRACELETS, NECKLACES, AND RINGS ARE ALSO USED TO REPRESENT THE CHAINS OF IMPRISONMENT.

RING: "A traditional symbol of infinity or eternity, the transposition of the CIRCLE into the real world of tangible, functional objects. In Greek and especially Roman antiquity, the privilege of wearing iron rings was reserved for prominent citizens. Priests of Jupiter were allowed to wear GOLD rings (the origin of the bishop's ring), and this privilege was subsequently extended to senators and KNIGHTS. There were also magical associations with rings..." [50]

"In the Middle Ages, rings came to symbolize betrothal (compare KNOTS) and MARRIAGE. Jeweled rings were also worn as amulets to ward off specific diseases (for example, carnelian against hemorrhaging or "spasm rings" against palsy). Since the time of Agrippa of Nettesheim (1486-1535), books of magic have contained instructions for making rings with every sort of secret power." [51]

"ENGAGEMENT & WEDDING RINGS"

The Egyptian pharaohs, however, are credited with being the first to use a ring in the form of a circular band as a symbol of eternity. The Egyptians regarded the circle, a shape with no beginning and no end, as a heavenly reminder that life, happiness, and love have no beginning or end.

By Roman times, it was an established tradition to give a ring, a symbol of the cycle of life and eternity, as a public pledge that the marriage contract between a man and woman would be honored. These early rings were made of iron, according to the accounts of Roman historian C. Plinius Secundus. Gold was introduced sometime in the second century A.D. Soon, the Christians adopted the custom, and the ring became an integral part of the marriage service. [52]

"Diamond held a particularly regal position at this time. It was one of the rarest and costliest of gems. And it was prized above other gems for marriage because of its unique properties and the many special powers attributed to it." [53]

"The Allure of Diamond:

Diamond, nature's hardest substance -- uniquely able to resist fire and steel and therefore all of man's early efforts to alter it -- epitomized unyielding power and invincible strength." [54]

"Legends of the diamond's mythical properties have been passed along for centuries. Hundreds of years before Christ, in India, where diamonds were first discovered, the diamond was valued even more for its strength and magic than its extraordinary beauty.

The diamond was thought to protect its wearer from snakes, fire, poison, illness, thieves, and all the combined forces of evil." [55]

As the gemstone of the zodiac House of Aries, symbolized by the Ram, the diamond was believed by ancient astrologers to be powerful for people born under the planet Mars.

They thought the diamond could provide fortitude, strength of mind, and continued love in marriage and ward off Witchcraft, poisons, and nightmares.

Each culture has prized the diamond for its unique properties. The Romans believed a diamond worn against the skin of their left arm would help them remain brave and daring in battle and give them strength over their enemies. An ancient passage reads: 'He who carries a diamond on the left side shall be hardly and manly; it will guard him from accidents to the limbs; nevertheless a good diamond will lose its power and virtue if worn by one who is incontinent, or drunken.' Another Roman practice was to set diamonds in fine steel, which would serve as a charm against insanity. [56]

Hindus, Chinese & Italians all attached special powers to the diamond.

"There is a catch, however, to the powers associated with it -- some believe that one must find the diamond "naturally" to experience its magic, that it loses its power if acquired by purchase. However, when offered as a pledge of love or friendship, its powers return!" [57]

The Middle Ages Set the Stage for Betrothal Traditions:
"In 1477, we find one of the first recorded accounts of the use of diamond in a betrothal ring." [58]

"Diamond crystals look like two pyramids joined together base-to-base. From the time of the Pharaohs, the shape of the pyramid was identified with power, strength, and mystery, so the 'pyramidal' shape of the diamond crystal itself may have added to the diamond's allure, the mystery and power identified with it. The very shape of the natural diamond crystal may have made it all the more attractive as the choice to symbolize the power of love and marriage." [59]

"...the Puritans, rebelling against Church ritual, unsuccessfully attempted to abolish the wedding ring. This test of tradition ultimately provided that the symbolism surrounding the custom of the wedding ring was too powerful to be destroyed." [60]

WHEN TODAY'S BRIDE RECEIVES HER ENGAGEMENT AND WEDDING RINGS, SHE WILL BECOME CONNECTED TO MEN AND WOMEN IN LOVE IN BOTH PAST AND FUTURE GENERATIONS. SHE WILL BECOME PART OF A TRADITION OF LOVE THAT HAS SPANNED CENTURIES. [61]

DICTIONARY OF SYMBOLS

GOLD: "...Gold jewelry was believed to ward off magic spells (especially when combined with PRECIOUS STONES). However, wearing gold jewelry was not allowed everywhere (See Rings). Gold was widely regarded as embodying the powers of the EARTH, and although it had virtually no practical value, it was always associated with higher powers and the gods. In many ancient civilizations, gold was reserved for producing sacred articles and ruler symbols. The "golden calf" of the Bible (Exodus 32: 1-24), a symbol of the "idolatry" of the northern Israelites, was not the image of a calf but of a Bull; Moses destroyed it. In ancient China, gold (chin), the solar metal, symbolized the principle of yang, the dualistic complement of Yin (whose metal was silver)." [62]

IRON: "Within the entire history of civilization, iron has been put to use only relatively recently; in myths of the ages of the EARTH, it represents the last stage in a progression that began with the GOLDEN AGE. Iron is an attribute of the god of war, MARS (Greek Aries), and the REDDISH COLOR of rust suggests that of BLOOD. In the ancient world, it was believed to be a metal of which demons and evil spirits were afraid; for this reason, many people wore iron RINGS and amulets, a practice that the Church found necessary to forbid as late as the seventh century after Christ." [63]

LEAD: "Viewed in antiquity as a metal with magic powers, lead tablets that had been scratched curses upon one's enemies were thought to be particularly effective. Thin plates of lead were worn over the chest as protection against magic spells, especially demonic love - spells." [64]

SILVER: "One of the "noble" metals, like GOLD, generally associated with the MOON itself or lunar deities, valued somewhat less than gold. In ancient Mexico, silver was called 'the white excrement of the gods' and was also thought of as the moon god's terrestrial counterpart (or feces). Silver was popularly believed to ward off demons." [65]

When I first wrote the book "Be Ye Holy," I went to the marketplace looking for examples. While shopping, I decided to look at jewelry for this project. The items mentioned here were found in 1995 in various stores.

GUARDIAN ANGELS: Angels guide you through the days and brighten your life. Keep an angel by your side, for dreams ride upon their wings.

THE CELESTIAL FIVE: This jewelry was found in a Christian Bookstore.
1. Angel of Protection: Protection & Guidance
2. Angel of Success: Provides the energy to be successful
3. Angel of Happiness: Brings on good times & joy
4. Angel of Love: Romance, Love, Great Relations
5. Angel of Wisdom: Knowledge, Decision-making

The concept of guardian angels, spiritual beings assigned to protect and guide individuals, has roots in ancient cultures and religions. Here's a brief overview of its history:

Ancient Roots:
• Pagan Beliefs: Many ancient cultures, including the Greeks, Romans, and Egyptians, believed in tutelary spirits or deities who watched over individuals or groups.
• Zoroastrianism: In this Persian religion, the concept of Fravashi, a spiritual guardian, is closely linked to the idea of a personal protector.

Judaism:
• Old Testament: While not explicitly mentioned, the idea of divine protection and guidance is present throughout the Old Testament.
• Rabbinic Literature: Rabbinic texts discuss the concept of a guardian angel, often referred to as a "malak" or "shemir."

Christianity:
• New Testament: The New Testament doesn't explicitly mention guardian angels but refers to angels as messengers and protectors.
• Early Christian Thought: Early Christian theologians and writers, such as Origen and Augustine, fully developed the idea of guardian angels.
• Medieval Period: The belief in guardian angels became widespread during the medieval period, with saints and religious figures often depicted with guardian angels.

Modern Times:
• Catholicism: The Catholic Church officially recognizes the belief in guardian angels, and the feast of the Guardian Angels is celebrated on October 2nd.
• Protestantism: While some Protestant denominations embrace the concept of guardian angels, others are more skeptical.
• Popular Culture: Guardian angels have been popularized in literature, film, and television, often portrayed as benevolent figures who intervene in human affairs.

It's important to note that the specific beliefs and practices related to guardian angels vary across different religions and cultural traditions. While some people may believe in a literal guardian angel, others may interpret the concept metaphorically or symbolically.

2 Corinthians 11:12 NLT: <u>*But I will continue doing what I have always done. This will undercut those who are looking for an opportunity to boast that their work is just like ours.*</u>

2 Corinthians 11:13 NLT: <u>*These people are false apostles. They are deceitful workers who disguise themselves as apostles of Christ.*</u>

2 Corinthians 11:14 NLT: <u>*But I am not surprised! Even Satan disguises himself as an angel of light.*</u>

2 Corinthians 11:15 NLT: <u>*So, it is no wonder that his servants also disguise themselves as servants of righteousness. In the end they will get the punishment their wicked deeds deserve.*</u>

MEDICINE WHEEL:
The circle that links all of life by wearing the wheel is thought to bring good fortune and ward off evil spirits.

North: Gives wisdom counsel
South: Reminds you when to trust
East: Guides you to your most significant challenges
West: Leads you to your truth

The Medicine Wheel holds profound spiritual significance for many Indigenous cultures, particularly North America. It symbolizes the interconnectedness of all things and the cyclical nature of life.

Essential spiritual meanings:
- **Circle:** The circle represents the universe, the Earth, and the individual. It symbolizes wholeness, completeness, and the eternal cycle of life. It reminds us that we are all connected and part of something greater than ourselves.
- **Four Directions:** The four directions (East, South, West, and North) represent the four elements (air, fire, water, and Earth), the four seasons, and the four stages of life (childhood, youth, adulthood, and elderhood). Each direction has its spiritual energy and teaches us different lessons about life.
- **Center:** The center of the wheel represents the spirit, the self, and the connection to all things. It is the source of power and wisdom and reminds us to connect with our inner selves and higher power.
- **Spokes:** The spokes radiating from the center connect the center to the four directions, symbolizing the flow of energy and the balance of all things. They remind us to balance our physical, emotional, mental, and spiritual selves.

The Medicine Wheel can be used for spiritual practices:
- **Healing:** The Medicine Wheel can heal the body, mind, and spirit. Each direction is associated with specific healing properties, and focusing on each can address different aspects of their well-being.

- **Meditation:** The Medicine Wheel can be used as a focus for meditation, helping to center the mind and connect with the spiritual self.
- **Ceremony:** The Medicine Wheel is often used in ceremonies and rituals, such as the Sun Dance, to honor the sacred and connect with the natural world.
- **Self-reflection:** The Medicine Wheel can be used as a tool for self-reflection, helping one understand one's strengths and weaknesses and identify areas for growth.

The Medicine Wheel is a powerful symbol that can be used in many ways. It reminds us of the interconnectedness of all things and the importance of living in harmony with the natural world.

DREAM CATCHER: Both bad and good descended from the heavens. The bad dreams were trapped in the web and held until the early morning sun evaporated them with dew. Good dreams filtered through the web into the sleeping person. A dream catcher is a handmade object from the Ojibwe people of North America. It consists of a willow hoop with a woven web, often decorated with feathers and beads.

Symbolism and Purpose:
- **Protection:** The dream catcher is believed to protect sleeping people from bad dreams and nightmares.
- **Good Dreams:** The web is said to catch bad dreams, while good dreams pass through the center and down the feathers to the sleeper.
- **Circle of Life:** The circular shape represents the circle of life, the journey of the sun and moon, and the interconnectedness of all things.
- **Spider Web:** The web is often associated with the spider, symbolizing creativity, patience, and protection.

How to Use a Dream Catcher:
- **Placement:** Traditionally, dream catchers are hung above a bed or cradle, where the morning sunlight can reach them.
- **Intention:** Set your intention for the dream catcher to protect you from negative energies and bring you positive dreams.

- **Maintenance:** Clean your dream catcher regularly with a feather duster or smoke cleansing.

Beyond the Traditional:
- **Symbol of Unity:** Dream catchers symbolize unity and hope for many people, regardless of their cultural background.
- **Personal Expression:** They can be customized with colors, beads, and feathers to reflect individual preferences and beliefs.
- **Decorative Art:** Dream catchers are often used as decorative items in homes and gardens.

Important Note: While dream catchers have become popular worldwide, it's crucial to remember their cultural significance. I am providing this information to help you be aware of the spiritual dangers involved in what seems innocent, unique, and beautiful.

SPIRIT BEAR:
Native American's classic "Power Animal" of protection and well-being! The bear, said to be the most powerful, will help you reach your goals and gain strength.

Why are they called "Spirit Bears"?
The name "Spirit Bear" comes from the First Nations people of the region, who have deep spiritual connections to these bears. They believe the Spirit Bear symbolizes purity and power and is significant in their cultural traditions.

Wear the Spirit Bear and feel the magic.

Fortune beads, also known as prayer beads or rosary beads, are used in various religious and spiritual practices worldwide. They are typically made of wood, stone, glass, or other materials and are strung together to form a necklace or bracelet.

The beads count repetitions of prayers, mantras, or other sacred texts. They can also be used as a meditation aid, helping to focus the mind and promote mindfulness. In some cultures, fortune beads are believed to have protective or healing properties.

There are many fortune beads, each with unique symbolism and significance.

Some of the most common types include:
- **Mala beads:** These are used in Hinduism, Buddhism, Sikhism, Jainism, and other Indian religions. They typically consist of 108 beads and are considered sacred in these traditions.
- **Rosary beads:** These are used in Catholicism and other Christian denominations. They usually consist of 59 beads, divided into ten called decades. Each decade is separated by a larger bead called a decade bead.
- **Tasbih beads:** These are used in Islam. They typically consist of 99 beads, representing the 99 names of Allah.
- **Prayer beads:** These are used in various other religions and spiritual traditions. Depending on the specific tradition, they can vary in size, shape, and number of beads.

Fortune beads are a versatile and powerful tool that can be used for various purposes. Whether you are looking to deepen your spiritual practice, improve your focus and concentration, or find a way to connect with your inner self, fortune beads can be a valuable aid.

When you rely on objects instead of Adonai, you say those items are more powerful. This violates the 1st Commandment: HAVE NO OTHER GODS.

The color of fortune beads can vary widely depending on the culture, religion, and specific purpose of the beads. However, certain colors are commonly associated with particular meanings or intentions:

- Black: Often associated with protection, grounding, and transformation.
- Brown: Represents stability, grounding, and connection to the Earth.
- Green: Symbolizes growth, renewal, prosperity, and healing.
- Red: Associated with passion, energy, vitality, and courage.
- Blue: Often linked to peace, tranquility, calmness, and spiritual awareness.
- Purple: Represents spirituality, wisdom, creativity, and royalty.

- White: Symbolizes purity, innocence, clarity, and new beginnings.
- Yellow: Associated with optimism, joy, intelligence, and creativity.

It's important to note that the meaning of colors can vary across different cultures and spiritual traditions. Some people may choose beads based on personal preference or aesthetic appeal, while others may select them based on their specific intentions or beliefs.

Tie one or more fortune beads on your wrist, ankle, or neck. Legend has it that your fortune will come true when it wears out and falls off.

DOLPHIN: Dolphins have guided sailors to new and distant lands for centuries. Let the Dolphin be the guiding force in your life.

LEGACY "WISH" COLLECTION: Heavenly Enchantment joins the world of magic, mystery, and fantasy. Precious Charms of Mystical figures are believed to bring good luck and grant wishes. May all your dreams come true!

What you have been reading is what was on the packages of the different items. Satan puts things out in the open through advertising, yet we ignore the facts. Power Animals is another form of spiritism.

POWER ANIMALS: Power animals, also known as spirit animals or totem animals, are animal guides that can provide protection, guidance, and healing. They can appear in dreams, meditations, or even in nature.

How to Connect with Your Power Animal:
1. **Meditation:** Find a quiet place to meditate and focus on your breath. Visualize a specific animal or allow an image to come to you.
2. **Dream Journaling:** Keep a dream journal to record animal encounters, whether symbolic or literal.
3. **Nature Walks:** Spend time in nature and pay attention to the animals you encounter.
4. **Shamanic Journey:** Work with a shaman or use guided meditations to journey to the spirit world and meet your power animal.

Standard Power Animals and Their Meanings:
- **Bear:** Strength, protection, and healing
- **Eagle:** Vision, wisdom, and courage
- **Wolf:** Loyalty, intuition, and community
- **Snake:** Transformation, healing, and wisdom
- **Deer:** Grace, gentleness, and intuition

MAGICAL TOUCH CRYSTAL:

Legend has it that Merlin the magician discovered the mystical touch crystal and its great soothing powers many years ago. When the crystal is touched, its soft, warm glow gives an immediate feeling of inner peace and tranquility. Now, you can discover the power of the mystical touch crystal and enjoy the peaceful, ever-changing colors it possesses.

The Belief:

Many believe crystals possess unique energies that can positively impact physical, emotional, and spiritual well-being. These beliefs often stem from ancient practices and cultural traditions. **Some common beliefs include:**
- **Energy Healing:** Crystals are thought to interact with the body's energy field, promoting balance and harmony.
- **Emotional Healing:** Certain crystals are believed to alleviate stress, anxiety, and depression.
- **Physical Healing:** Some people use crystals to aid in recovery from illness or injury.
- **Spiritual Growth:** Crystals are often used in meditation and spiritual practices to enhance connection with higher consciousness.

The Science:

While many value crystal healing, no scientific evidence supports these claims. The alleged benefits of crystals are often attributed to the placebo effect, where belief in a treatment can lead to perceived improvements.

This is what people are told to get them to embrace occult ideas.

However, it's important to note that crystals can have a positive psychological impact. Choosing a crystal, holding it, and meditating with it can be a calming and grounding experience. This can improve mood, reduce stress, and a sense of well-being.

Powerstone belief is that specific stones and crystals possess unique properties that can positively impact the wearer's mind, body, and spirit. These stones, often referred to as "power stones," are believed to have the ability to heal, protect, and enhance various aspects of life.

Common Beliefs and Practices:
- **Healing Properties:** Different stones are associated with specific healing properties, such as physical ailments, emotional imbalances, or spiritual blockages.
- **Energy Absorption and Amplification:** Some believe power stones can absorb negative energy and amplify positive energy, leading to overall well-being.
- **Meditation and Mindfulness:** Power stones are often used as tools for meditation and mindfulness practices, helping to focus the mind and promote relaxation.
- **Protection and Luck:** Certain stones offer protection from harm and negative influences and bring good luck.
- **Astrological Significance:** Some people believe power stones can be chosen based on their astrological signs to enhance their strengths and mitigate weaknesses.

Important Considerations:
- **Scientific Evidence:** While many value power stone beliefs, no scientific evidence supports their claims.
- **Personal Experience:** The effectiveness of power stones often depends on individual belief and experience.
- **Ethical Sourcing:** Choosing ethically sourced power stones is essential to ensure they do not contribute to environmental damage or human rights abuses.

Popular Power Stones and Their Beliefs:
- **Amethyst:** Associated with peace, tranquility, and spiritual awareness.
- **Quartz:** Believed to enhance clarity, focus, and energy.
- **Rose Quartz:** Often used for love, compassion, and self-love.

- **Obsidian:** Known for protection, grounding, and cutting through illusions.
- **Turquoise:** Associated with good fortune, protection, and communication.

Satan, also known as evil demon forces, wants humanity to be deceived and will promote anything and everything to keep an individual from turning to Adonai and trusting Him. In desperation, when in pain, we reach out to the occult, not knowing the actual entrapment is to cause a violation of the Commandments once again.

The New World Order requires a significant change in the Christian belief system to usher in the New Age. Therefore, we must realize that one goal of NAM (New Age Movement) is to destroy the Word of God. The ideas of SPIRITUAL ENLIGHTENMENT commonly used follow:

"INTRODUCTORY ESSAY: AN OVERVIEW OF THE NEW AGE MOVEMENT NEW AGE ENCYCLOPEDIA, FIRST EDITION"

Tools for Spiritual Transformation: "An overwhelming number of New Agers, however, have not had the isolated mystical experience but have been transformed over time by using one of the New Age tools within a New Age setting. Change might start with rebirthing, meditation, wearing a crystal, participating in an intensive seminar, or receiving healing from any of what may appear to be an endless variety of New Age healers." [66]

Swedenborgianism: "Swendenborg became the first to state the nebular hypothesis of the universe's origin (that it evolved from a hot, gaseous nebula), and, as a metallurgist, he pioneered the development of crystallography and mineralogy. But he rejected his scientific pursuits to spend the last decades of his life in intimate communion with what he claimed were angels." [67]

Theosophical Offshoots: "I AM Religious Movement emphasized the importance of light (a common element in many reports of mystical experience) and added an emphasis upon the spiritual (occult) significance of color. The attention paid to color, especially as experienced in the light of gems, underlies the love of crystals in recent decades." [68]

THE FACTS ON HOLISTIC HEALTH AND THE NEW MEDICINE, CAN YOU TRUST YOUR DOCTOR?

What is crystal healing/crystal work?

Crystal healing, currently one of the most popular New Age practices, involves using a supposed 'power' inherent in crystals to heal, develop psychic abilities, contact spirits, and achieve other New Age goals. Crystals supposedly contain the ability to focus and direct psychic energies for healing and other occult pursuits.

Crystal work is a form of animism in which inanimate objects are held to possess spiritual powers that may be contacted, utilized, or directed. But in animism, any supernatural power that is contacted originates from the spirit world. Thus, crystals per se have no magical powers and only become an implement behind which spirits may work. When pressed, most crystal healers we have talked with concede that the power behind crystals is spiritistic.

Similar objects (amulets, magical stones, or gems) are also believed to possess magical properties. Still, one fact discounts this belief: Psychic abilities and powers remain once the implement is dispensed. In other words, these objects are only contact material–a disguise through which spirits work to gain influence over people's lives.

All divinatory methods utilize some principle object that becomes the focus and vehicle through which spirits work to serve the client and produce the needed answer to questions, character analysis, future prognostication, supernatural power, etc. Typical forms of divination and the objects they use include astrology (the horoscope chart); tarot (a deck of cards with symbols); I Ching (sticks, printed hexagrams); runes (dice); Ouija board (an alphabet planchette); radionics/psychometry (the diving rod, pendulum, "black box," etc.); palmistry (the hand); crystal-gazing (the crystal ball or crystal rock); metoscopy /physiognomy/ phrenology (the forehead, face, skull); geomancy (combinations of dots or points); water dowsing (the forked stick or other objects).

Is it logical to expect that mere pieces of paper bearing symbols (horoscopes), simple forked sticks, cards, hands, dice, letters of the alphabet, rocks, facial lines, or dots could ever supply supernatural power or miraculous information about a person or their future? Even the practitioners of these arts refer to 'supernatural influences' - to 'gods' and spirits who operate through these methods.

The potential problems arising from crystal healing include those of New Age Medicine in general: misdiagnosis, mistreatment, and occultic influence. [69]

"THE FACTS ON THE NEW AGE MOVEMENT"

"One major use involves the alleged focusing or directing of crystal energy for specific purposes, such as psychic healing, contact with spirits, or developing higher consciousness and psychic powers." [70]

"These objects themselves have no power. However, when used for occult purposes, they can become vehicles for spirits to work through, much like common wood (divining rod, Ouija board), cards or sticks (Tarot cards, I Ching)." [71]

Deuteronomy 18:9 NLT: "When you enter the land the LORD your God is giving you, be very careful not to imitate the detestable customs of the nations living there.

Deuteronomy 18:10 NLT: For example, never sacrifice your son or daughter as a burnt offering. And do not let your people practice fortune-telling, or use sorcery, or interpret omens, or engage in Witchcraft,

Deuteronomy 18:11 NLT: or cast spells, or function as mediums or psychics, or call forth the spirits of the dead.

Deuteronomy 18:12 NLT: Anyone who does these things is detestable to the LORD. It is because the other nations have done these detestable things that the LORD your God will drive them out ahead of you.

Deuteronomy 18:13 NLT: But you must be blameless before the LORD your God.

Deuteronomy 18:14 NLT: <u>*The nations you are about to displace consult sorcerers and fortune-tellers, but the LORD your God forbids you to do such things."*</u>

These scriptures mention nine abominations: human sacrifice, divination, an observer of times, an enchanter, a witch, a charmer, a consulter with familiar spirits, a wizard, and a necromancer.

Revelation 9:20 NLT: <u>*But the people who did not die in these plagues still refused to repent of their evil deeds and turn to God. They continued to worship demons and idols made of gold, silver, bronze, stone, and wood--idols that can neither see nor hear nor walk!*</u>

Revelation 9:21 NLT: <u>*And they did not repent of their murders or their Witchcraft or their sexual immorality or their thefts.*</u>

Revelation 18:23 NLT: <u>*The light of a lamp will never shine in you again. The happy voices of brides and grooms will never be heard in you again. For your merchants were the greatest in the world, and you deceived the nations with your sorceries.*</u>

Revelation 18:24 NLT: <u>*In your streets flowed the blood of the prophets and of God's holy people and the blood of people slaughtered all over the world."*</u>

This chapter has only scratched the surface. Throughout the series Victorious, I will delve into each holiday and its origins, inviting you to examine them critically.

Our responsibility is to be informed, teach, and expose what our society observes. It has been easy to embrace our heritage without questions.

Since the beginning of Christianity, the early church fathers compromised and incorporated paganism into the Christian Church.

It's crucial to understand that partaking in these pagan rituals and distancing yourself from Adonai may cause your prayers to go unheard.

When I first wrote Be Ye Holy, I didn't have the Internet. I researched each topic and talked to those involved in the occult.

Now, numerous videos are available about the origin of the holidays, along with other historical facts.

Exorcism is a religious or spiritual practice aimed at expelling evil spirits or demons from a person or place believed to be possessed. It is rooted in various cultures and religions throughout history, with rituals and beliefs varying across different traditions.

The way the world of darkness works is that they look at what you are wearing. They know that you are ignorant and will do everything within their power to call up spirits to destroy you.

I have seen Adonai deliver people from evil spirits, which is very serious. Don't ever play with the spirit world. Make sure your life aligns with the scriptures and Adonai's attributes.

Keep in mind that it is not your righteousness; it is His. Satan can't come close to those who honor and serve the Lord. He will use others; when that happens, distance yourself from the individual.

As you read this series, you will be able to recognize signs, symbols, words, ideas, etc., that are all around us. Never be afraid of what you learn. As you develop spiritually, the demons will be more fearful of you than you will ever be of them.

Chapter 4
What God Hates

I have heard that Jesus loves me and that Grace covers our sins all my life. What does that mean?

What is sin? The concept of sin varies across different religions, but it is often defined as a transgression against divine Law or a moral code. It can involve actions, thoughts, or words considered wrong or harmful to humanity.

In its most basic sense, Grace is unmerited favor—receiving something you don't deserve. In a religious context, it often refers to God's undeserved love and kindness. However, the concept of Grace extends beyond religion. It can be applied to any situation where someone receives kindness or forgiveness they haven't earned.

The things that God hates are called abominations in the scriptures.

Abomination is a noun that means something regarded with disgust or hatred. It can also refer to extreme disgust or hatred itself. For example, war could be considered an abomination, or someone might feel an abomination toward a particular crime.

The word abomination comes from the Old French abomination, which means "horror, repugnance, disgust." It is often used to describe something morally wrong or offensive.

The word "abomination" is used several times in the Bible, primarily in the Old Testament. It is often used to describe things considered morally wrong or offensive to God.

I am using the NLT for these scriptures to make them easier to understand. However, regardless of which version of the Bible you read, these scriptures have the same core meanings.

Deuteronomy 22:5 NLT: *"A woman shall not wear anything that pertains to a man, nor shall a man put on a woman's garment, for all who do so are an abomination to the LORD your God.*

For years, this Scripture has been a source of contention. The argument has waged over whether there is a difference in women's pants vs. men's pants. Researching the history of clothing will help you find this out.

The debate goes much further than that. One example in today's society is cross-dressing.

Cross-dressing refers to wearing clothes typically associated with a gender different from one's own. Here are some key points to consider:

There are several reasons for Cross-Dressing listed are some of the excuses or reasons why people might give cross-dress, including:
• **Self-expression:** It can be a way to express oneself creatively or explore different aspects of identity.
• **Sexual arousal:** For some, it may be a source of sexual pleasure or fantasy.
• **Comfort and enjoyment:** It might simply be a way to feel comfortable and happy.
• **Religious or cultural practices:** In some cultures, cross-dressing has historical or spiritual significance.
• **Gender Identity:** Cross-dressing is distinct from transgender identity. While some transgender individuals may cross-dress as part of their transition, others may not. Similarly, not all cross-dressers identify as transgender.

Adonai created a difference between males and females. His plan is perfect.

Women, I want to address the issue of wearing pants. Years ago, I had a panel discussion concerning women who used to wear pants and the spirit behind their choice of clothing. Women on the panel said they felt a spiritual transformation of equality and liberation when wearing pants.

I want to take you through the history of cross-dressing.

Only in the fourteenth century did little change in women's dress. "In the fourteenth century, there was a sudden realization that clothes, instead of mere wrappings, could be used to attract the attention, and influence the choice, of the other sex..." [1]

Women like Frances Anne (Fanny) Kemble, Amelia Jenks Bloomer, Elizabeth Smith Miller, and Elizabeth Cady Stanton would take action that would change women's lives forever. These would be instrumental in bringing change to hundreds who had suffered injustices due to the harsh laws that governed women. One such Law stated that a woman must continue to live with a man who had alcoholism, whether he supported her or not. If she left him, she could not take her children with her. The Law stated that the wife would lose everything if the husband died before she did. The Law also said that all money earned was the husband's. The initial motive behind the women's movement was sincere, and change was needed.

At the same time, America began fighting a tremendous spiritual battle. Satan became bold. Spiritism, a hidden practice, began to be used openly. (Spiritism is the practice of communication with the dead. The Bible refers to it as necromancy.) Satan is slick. Look how he set his trap. First, it brings injustices that cause hurt and confusion. Then, under the camouflage of turmoil, he introduced his system of change.

The following women played a significant role in American history.

FRANCES ANNE ("FANNY") KEMBLE (1809-1893) was perhaps the first actress to gain a national following. From London, her immediate success was due to playing

Shakespeare's Juliet from 1832 to 1834. She was the first woman to become a celebrity in the U.S. and Europe. Kemble was important to FEMINISTS for her independent lifestyle and early role in DRESS REFORM. Amelia Bloomer's 1849 defense of Kemble's fashion innovation drew attention to the new garment. [2]

AMELIA JENKS BLOOMER (1818-1894): Amelia Bloomer did not invent the costume, and while "bloomers" are strongly associated with women, Elizabeth Smith Miller created the new form of dress. [3]

(Amelia Jenks Bloomer was married, so the term "bloomers" is taken from her husband's name.)

"Indeed, it was through QUAKER attorney and newspaper editor Dexter Bloomer that Amelia Jenks came to be involved in the liberalizing issues of her era. They married in 1840 when she was twenty-two. Amelia Bloomer, a TEACHER until marriage, began writing articles for her husband's newspaper, especially on TEMPERANCE -- which was her chief lifelong interest." [4]

"...Amelia Bloomer was rather slow to accept FEMINISM, publishing her paper for a dozen years before she made public appearances with women's rights leaders, and then her speeches were devoted to the right of women to DIVORCE alcoholic husbands." [5]

Amelia was perhaps the first woman to edit a newspaper—certainly the first since the colonial era. The paper, the LILY, began publication in January 1846.

Amelia was probably at the 1848 SENECA FALLS women's rights meeting in New York State primarily as a reporter rather than a participant. She met Susan B. Anthony, Lucretia MOTT, and Elizabeth Cady STANTON. The following year, she branched out with her paper, an idea proposed by her temperance society.

"In 1849, Elizabeth Smith MILLER appeared in Seneca Falls wearing the new 'Turkish trousers'; Miller was the daughter of abolitionist Gerrit Smith, and it was he who was the most vocal advocate of the new style, arguing that men would better accept women if their appearance were less strikingly different." [6]

Elizabeth Smith Miller's cousin was the famous feminist Elizabeth Cady STANTON, who promoted the new style of trousers. She wore the trousers to the temperance meetings. Amelia BLOOMER reported the event in the LILY.

Interest in the new style doubled newspaper subscriptions, presumably by readers more interested in fashion than temperance.

Women like Susan B. Anthony, Paulina Wright Davis, Lucy Stone, Dr. Harriet Austin, and Fanny KEMBLE, along with many others, would follow suit in wearing the "Bloomers."

ELIZABETH CADY STANTON (1815-1902) "Elizabeth Cady was born in western New York State, where her family had long been locally influential. Like other girls of her era, it was only because of her ambition that she was educated; she studied Greek and Latin in books bought for her brother..." [7]

She was eleven years old when her brother Eleazer was accidentally killed. Judge Cady was so overcome with grief at the loss of his son and felt that a great injustice had been dealt him. He is quoted, "Oh my daughter, I wish you were a boy!" This statement would be said to her repeatedly with every significant accomplishment. What started as an innocent desire to help her grieving father overcome the death of her brother would usher many events, eventually leading to drastic changes in the lives of women.

In 1832, decades before colleges were open to women, Elizabeth attempted to enroll in Union College but was rejected. She took advantage of Emma Willard's Female Seminary in Troy, New York, the only superior secondary school available.

[During her stay, Elizabeth met] "Reverend Dr. Charles G. Finney, ex-president of Oberlin College and one of the most famous evangelists of the era. The Cady family belonged to the Scotch Presbyterian Church, and Elizabeth had been reared in a strong and gloomy Calvinist tradition." [8]

"...Elizabeth had questioned her nurse, 'Why is everything I like sin and everything I dislike commanded by God? I am so tired of that everlasting No! No! No! I suppose God will say 'no' to all we like in the next world.'" [9]

Elizabeth disagreed with the Rev. Finney and went to tell him. Within a short period afterward, she suffered from fear and eventually an emotional collapse. For six weeks, Elizabeth stayed with her father, her sister, and her brother-in-law, and religion was forbidden as a topic of conversation. She read Combe's Constitution of Man and Moral Philosophy during that time. After reading the book, she willingly traded religion for intellectual stimulation. (This book promotes ideas of the New Age Movement.)

On Thursday, May 10, 1840, Elizabeth Cady and Henry Stanton were married in a ceremony that became the talk of the town. It marked a new beginning, but the word "OBEY" was not used in their ceremony. She contended that their marriage was a partnership and not an ownership.

Greatly disturbed by the injustices of being born a woman, she quickly grew bitter. More than ever, she would fight for women's rights. The desire to destroy the laws governing women and to create change engulfed her. All she saw was cruelty and injustice.

Elizabeth was overwhelmed by Lucretia Mott, a Quaker. "...Lucretia Mott, who was some twenty years older than she and a liberal thinker who questioned religion, politics, and social reform. Her refusal to interpret the Scriptures literally or to accept any artificial creed impressed Elizabeth. " [10]

Therefore, Elizabeth sought her out at every opportunity to discuss her ideas about "new liberties" for women.

"If Susan B. Anthony was the chief organizer of the nineteenth-century women's movement, then Elizabeth Cady Stanton was its chief thinker. Moreover, Stanton led the movement for several years before Anthony's involvement: as the prime author of the DECLARATION OF RIGHTS OF WOMEN, she already had made a major contribution to women's history before Anthony ever appeared on the scene."

Stanton was president of the NATIONAL AMERICAN WOMAN SUFFRAGE ASSOCIATION from 1890-1892.

Stanton "...was motivated by an unusually profound ability to empathize..." [11]

Because of her childhood, she traced her activism to her attorney father's female clients, whose lives were affected by the Law's failure to treat them equally. "At the same time, Stanton's father was not supportive of her activism and once disinherited her; a judge later in life, he was more than a little judgmental. Their disagreements left her doubly depressed, for the problem was complicated by his grief for his only son, who had died young. Her insistence that she be addressed as Elizabeth Cady Stanton may have had partial motivation in proving to her father that a daughter could be as worthwhile as a son." [12]

"Though she never attended another suffrage convention after retiring from the presidency, Stanton's days of radical leadership were not over. As the suffrage movement grew increasingly conservative and ineffective, Stanton again turned to the pen rather than the platform." [13]

In August 1886, Elizabeth, expressing dissatisfaction with Christianity, proposed writing a new Bible to Frances Lord from London. Motivated to address and rectify perceived injustices toward women in the existing scriptures, Elizabeth began to outline the project, marking the initial steps toward a reimagined religious text.

Two weeks after publicizing her eightieth birthday in November 1895, Stanton shocked even feminists with the publication of Volume I of The Women's Bible. Elizabeth Cady Stanton's attack on traditional church teachings about the status of women, including the inequality within the church, provoked a violent storm.

She began working on the document in 1886 and planned to force women to question their religious convictions. Many women feared tampering with the Bible and withdrew, while others continued.

"Clara Bewick Colby became Elizabeth's staunch supporter in writing The Women's Bible. Like Elizabeth, she was convinced that women would never achieve equality until they freed themselves from religion and the church." [14]

In a statement concerning women's elevation and proper position, her commentary states.

Genesis 1:27-28: "We have in these texts a plain declaration of the existence of the feminine element in the Godhead, equal in power and glory with the masculine. The Heavenly Mother and Father! 'God created man in his image, male and female.' Thus, Scripture, science, and philosophy declare the eternity and equality of sex." [15]

Theodore Parker and William Henry Channing first became aware of the concept of a Heavenly Mother. However, Elizabeth often used it when asked to say Grace at the table.

"Mrs. Stanton's religious beliefs went so far toward the unconventional as to include a sort of Freudian analysis before the coming of Freud. She contended that the feminine side of humanity, being holy and affectional, evolves the masculine God, as each sex worships its opposite..." [16]

"To people who had been taught that the Bible was the direct and divinely inspired word of God, they classified The Woman's Bible as heresy. Most of the reviews strongly opposed the ideas Elizabeth and her co-commentators presented. But I had gone through three American and two English editions within a year."[17]

It was the carefully researched argument against women's subordinate position in religion that, like the Revolution, was more reasonable than its inflammatory title implied.

"Reverend Anna Howard Shaw and others moved a resolution in the 1896 NAWSA convention disassociating the organization from the book, and despite Anthony's impassioned plea, the motion passed. However, this hailstorm of outrage gave Stanton no pause, and in 1898, she added a second volume." [18]

Volume I covered the Pentateuch (Genesis—Deuteronomy). The second, published in 1898, dealt with the rest of the Old and New Testaments, from Joshua to Revelation.

Clara B. Neyman, Louisa Southworth, Lucinda B. Chandler, Phebe A. Hanaford, Matilda Joslyn Gage, Frances Ellen Burr, and Ellen Dietrich all shared Elizabeth's convictions about religion and the scriptures. They helped provide some of the commentary.

Elizabeth was neither surprised nor discouraged by much of the adverse reaction. She was pleased to see many people reading and discussing The Woman's Bible. Having only provoked women to think, she was successful.

The spiritual condition of the women responsible for the drastic changes in history, both in Law and dress reform, is obvious.

For the first two years, women faced tremendous pressure regarding Turkish trousers. The majority of the women chose to return to the customary dress. However, some refused.

The history of the "BLOOMERS" and Amelia Bloomer can be found at the Smithsonian Institute in Washington, D.C. The London News illustrated the Bloomers on September 27, 1851, worn by Amelia Jenks Bloomer (the picture shows her in the new costume and haircut).

"Its (referring to the bloomers) comfort was undeniable, but its adoption by women identified with radical tendencies -- women who shingled their hair to be en rapport with their skirts -- sealed its doom. For the people of that day were unprepared for the short-skirted, short-haired women..." [19]

"More than any other era in American history, World War I was a turning point. The five years between 1916 and 1921 made a more dramatic difference than any other similarly brief period of the world's history, and nowhere can this be seen as clearly as in women's lives. In 1916, their roles were still largely defined by the standards of the Victorian age; by 1921, they had the vote, and the FLAPPER of the Roaring Twenties symbolized their liberation." [20]

FLAPPERS: The term for women in the 1920s who, by changes in dress and lifestyle, transformed forever the image of women in the Western world. Motivated in part by their disillusioning and yet confidence-building experiences during World War I, "flappers" in both Britain and America were primarily known for "bobbing" the long hair that women had historically worn piled heavily on their heads, cutting it instead into a short, straight style that required little care. They also adopted skirts that rose above the ankle and then above the knee, shockingly abandoning the virtues of modesty that had kept skirts to female feet for centuries.

Petticoats, HATS, high-top shoes, and corsets were rejected. Sleeves were cut, too, for the key to flappers' apparel was casual maintenance and ease of athletics, as women adopted sports, especially swimming, that previously had been male preserves. In addition to changes in dress, flappers prided themselves on adopting male habits in alcohol and cigarette use; they drove cars, danced newly suggestive dances to revolutionary jazz music, and frequented the new moving picture houses.

While many associate the "flapper" with the flapping movements of the era's dances, especially the Charleston, the word was earlier used in Britain to denote a fledgling young woman. It developed disparaging connotations in the twenties, as the British withheld the vote from women younger than thirty. There and in America, however, no other generation of young women has made such significant change in such a short time with such dramatic implications for women's history as did the "flapper." [21]

Before long, the NINETEENTH AMENDMENT was passed. Women everywhere began to make the same lifestyle changes, just like the flappers. "Other changes occurred that were at the same time conspicuous and profoundly subtle: women shortened their skirts and bobbed their hair; they began going to movies, smoking cigarettes, driving cars, and using BIRTH CONTROL. In dozens of ways, young women's lives became more like those of men, and often, these changes were motivated by a profound cynicism and a rejection of Authority based on wartime experience. World War I was an extremely bloody war that seemingly wrought no genuine good (especially after the U.S. refused to join the League of Nations). It brought complex changes to ordinary people and how they lived their lives. The Western world, especially its women, would never return to the innocence of prewar days." [22]

A woman's first day at work might mean that naked and shivering under a dressing gown, she submitted to a factory's routine physical examination. Such an exam may have been a rude beginning for a woman's work life, something dehumanizing and intimidating. It was the first indication of the total invasion of privacy that war work entailed. Most factories dictated how a woman must clothe herself. The objective was to ensure safety, but for women who had never appeared in public wearing anything other than skirts, the adjustment to dressing like men was a profound change. Much media attention was given to this Revolution. While most of it was written in the determinedly shallow style so popular with World War II editors, the public nonetheless seemed to grasp that this transformation in dress represented a severe and permanent change in women's roles.

Wearing male clothing was a genuine liberation for women—ironically, it was brought about by a need to conform.

Dress codes were enforced even at plants that did not insist on uniforms. Slacks and sturdy, low-heeled shoes were mandatory. Similar regulations were enforced on other aspects of feminine appearance. A decade or two earlier, bobbed hair was controversial, but now women found that long tresses were a factory taboo. If her hair were not as short as a man's, it had to be pushed under a turban. Management would assume no risk that she could be scalped by whirling machinery. [23]

Numerous articles have been written by fashion designers and consultants repeatedly stating that women have adopted men's styles. Below is a list of terms and a description of the clothing article. These quotes are directly from the book.

"THE ENCYCLOPEDIA OF FASHION" GAUCHO PANTS: "Pants adapted from the wide-bottomed, mid-calf divided skirts worn by the South American COWBOY. Saint Laurent popularized gauchos in the 1960s when they were worn with boots, shirts, and wide belts with large silver buckles." [24]

JEANS: "From Genes, the French for Genoa, Italy, a port where sailors wore sturdy work pants. Jeans are strong cotton cloth originally loomed in Nimes, France, and are also the name for pants made from that cloth. During the 1850s, Levi Strauss introduced denim jeans as workwear for gold miners in San Francisco, California. They became fashionable in the 1950s in the U.S.A." [25]

PANTS: (U.K.: trousers) "Outer garments which cover the body from the waist to the ankles in two separate leg sections. Pants have been worn by MEN, in one form or another, since ancient times." [26]

"...Pants were not commonly worn by women until the 1920s." [27]

"During World War II, women taking over men's work wore pants in the factories and fields, but after the war, the only fashionable pants were BERMUDA SHORTS, PEDAL PUSHERS. And TOREADOR PANTS, all worn as part of casual dress. The real pants revolution came in the 1960s, with UNISEX FASHIONS, though even at this time, women wearing pants were often refused entry to restaurants, and the whole subject was one heated debate." [28]

UNISEX: "Clothes designed to be worn by either sex, popular in the 1960s and 1970s. Unisex garments included pants, jackets, WAISTCOATS, and shirts. The unisex look emerged as men wore floral patterns and women adopted men's garments. Although novel then, the idea has been accepted in fashion since the early 1980s." [29]

SO EITHER WOMEN ARE WEARING MEN'S PANTS OR MEN ARE WEARING WOMEN'S.

Deuteronomy 22:5 The woman shall not wear that which pertaineth unto a man; neither shall a man put on a woman's garment: for all that do so are abomination unto the LORD thy God.

I realize that this Scripture does not say DON'T WEAR PANTS. This Scripture tells us not to wear anything that pertains to the opposite sex.

"THE AMERICAN COLLEGE DICTIONARY" PERTAIN: to have reference or relation; relate; to belong or be connected as a part, adjunct, possession, attribute, etc.

"Nelson's ILLUSTRATED BIBLE DICTIONARY" ABOMINATION: Anything that offends the spiritual, religious, or moral sense of a person and causes extreme disgust, hatred, or loathing.

Most of the Hebrew words translated as "abomination" have the meaning of "impure," "filthy and unclean"–that which is foul-smelling and objectionable to a holy God.

Some people will say this is not a salvational issue.

Why would anyone who loves God take part in what God hates?

Leviticus 18:20-26 NLT: "Do not defile yourself by having sexual intercourse with your neighbor's wife. "Do not permit any of your children to be offered as a sacrifice to Molech, for you must not bring shame on the name of your God. I am the LORD. "Do not practice homosexuality, having sex with another man as with a woman. It is a detestable sin. "A man must not defile himself by having sex with an animal. And a woman must not offer herself to a male animal to have intercourse with it. This is a perverse act. "Do not defile yourselves in any of these ways, for the people I am driving out before you have defiled themselves in all these ways. Because the entire land has become defiled, I am punishing the people who live there. I will cause the land to vomit them out. You must obey all my decrees and regulations. You must not commit any of these detestable sins.

This applies both to native-born Israelites and to the foreigners living among you.

Leviticus 20:12-16 NLT: "If a man has sex with his daughter-in-law, both must be put to death. They have committed a perverse act and are guilty of a capital offense. "If a man practices homosexuality, having sex with another man as with a woman, both men have committed a detestable act. They must both be put to death, for they are guilty of a capital offense. "If a man marries both a woman and her mother, he has committed a wicked act. The man and both women must be burned to death to wipe out such wickedness from among you. "If a man has sex with an animal, he must be put to death, and the animal must be killed. "If a woman presents herself to a male animal to have intercourse with it, she and the animal must both be put to death. It would help if you killed both, for they are guilty of a capital offense.

Deuteronomy 7:25-26 NLT: "You must burn their idols in fire, and you must not covet the silver or gold that covers them. You must not take it or it will become a trap to you, for it is detestable to the LORD your God. Do not bring any detestable objects into your home, for then you will be destroyed, just like them. You must utterly detest such things, for they are set apart for destruction.

Deuteronomy 12:29-32 NLT: "When the LORD your God cuts off from before you the nations which you go to dispossess, and you displace them and dwell in their land, "take heed to yourself that you are not ensnared to follow them, after they are destroyed from before you, and that you do not inquire after their gods, saying, 'How did these nations serve their gods? I also will do likewise.' "You shall not worship the LORD your God in that way; for every abomination to the LORD which He hates they have done to their gods; for they burn even their sons and daughters in the fire to their gods. "Whatever I command you, be careful to observe it; you shall not add to it nor take away from it.

Deuteronomy 18:9-14 NLT: "When you come into the land which the LORD your God is giving you, you shall not learn to follow the abominations of those nations. "There shall not be found among you anyone who makes his son or his daughter pass through the fire, or one who practices witchcraft, or a soothsayer, or one who interprets omens, or a sorcerer, "or one who conjures spells, or a medium, or a spiritist, or one who calls up the dead. "For all who do these things are an abomination to the LORD, and because of these abominations the LORD your God drives them out from before you. "You shall be blameless before the LORD your God. "For these nations which you will dispossess listened to soothsayers and diviners; but as for you, the LORD your God has not appointed such for you.

Deuteronomy 25:16 NLT: "For all who do such things, all who behave unrighteously, are an abomination to the LORD your God.

Deuteronomy 27:14-16 NLT: "And the Levites shall speak with a loud voice and say to all the men of Israel: 'Cursed is the one who makes a carved or molded image, an abomination to the LORD, the work of the hands of the craftsman, and sets it up in secret.' "And all the people shall answer and say, 'Amen!' 'Cursed is the one who treats his father or his mother with contempt.' "And all the people shall say, 'Amen!'

Proverbs 6:16-19 NLT: There are six things the LORD hates--no, seven things he detests: haughty eyes, a lying tongue, hands that kill the innocent, a heart that plots evil, feet that race to do wrong, a false witness who pours out lies, a person who sows discord in a family.

Proverbs 15:26-29 NLT: The thoughts of the wicked are an abomination to the LORD, But the words of the pure are pleasant. He who is greedy for gain troubles his own house, But he who hates bribes will live. The heart of the righteous studies how to answer, But the mouth of the wicked pours forth evil. The LORD is far from the wicked, But He hears the prayer of the righteous.

Proverbs 28:9-10 NLT: One who turns away his ear from hearing the Law, Even his prayer is an abomination. Whoever causes the upright to go astray in *an evil way, He himself will fall into his own pit; But the blameless will inherit good.*

Isaiah 1:13-16 NLT: Bring no more futile sacrifices; Incense is an abomination to Me. The New Moons, the sabbaths, and the calling of assemblies--I cannot endure iniquity and the sacred meeting. Your New Moons and your appointed feasts My soul hates; They are a trouble to Me, I am weary of bearing them. When you spread out your hands, I will hide My eyes from you; Even though you make many prayers, I will not hear. Your hands are full of blood. "Wash yourselves, make yourselves clean; Put away the evil of your doings from before My eyes. Cease to do evil,

Revelation 21:27 NLT: But there shall by no means enter it anything that defiles, or causes an abomination or a lie, but only those who are written in the Lamb's Book of Life.

HOW DOES THIS AFFECT US TODAY?

SATAN HAS ALWAYS OPPOSED GOD. By ignoring God's basic foundations, lives become disastrous without structure.

God won't hear the prayers of any individual who opposes His commandments. How do people oppose the commandments of God? By picking and choosing which ones you want to obey.

In the Christian world, the first four commandments are constantly violated, and when we need strength and direction because of our defiance, God does not hear us in prayer.

Deuteronomy 22:5 is only one issue that Satan has used to mock God. You might ask, how? Those who analyze and debate the scriptures then determine the importance of an issue and set themselves up as gods.

The New Age Movement teaches that everyone must be transformed or enlightened. It teaches that everyone must obtain a higher consciousness, resulting in full "god-realization."

They believe that to gain this type of transformation, we need to take three steps:

1) Realize all is one, 2) all is God, and 3) we are God.

As gods, they believe they have a right to determine their course.

They seek out only what they feel will assist them in higher consciousness. Techniques that help produce higher consciousness include:
- Participating in potential human seminars.
- Spending time in a flotation tank with sensory deprivation.
- Physical and breathing exercises accompany meditation.
- Engaging in creative visualization is when one's mind pictures the reality of what one desires in life to be.

They also use yoga, reflexology, iridology, acupuncture, martial arts, and therapeutic touch to raise consciousness levels. Various objects, such as rock crystals, pyramids, colors, flower essences, etc., are also used.

The New Age movement is a diverse and eclectic collection of beliefs and practices that emerged in the mid-20th century. While there is no single authority or set of doctrines that define it, some core themes and beliefs are commonly associated with the New Age:

- **Holism:** The belief that the mind, body, and spirit are interconnected and should be approached as a whole. This emphasis on holistic health and well-being is a central tenet of the New Age movement.
- **Spirituality:** The belief in a personal connection to the divine or a higher power, often expressed through meditation, yoga, or other spiritual practices. New Age spirituality usually draws on elements from various religions and philosophies, including Buddhism, Hinduism, and Native American traditions.

- **Self-realization:** The belief in the individual's inherent worth and potential. New Age practices often focus on personal growth, self-discovery, and developing one's spiritual and psychic abilities.
- **Positive thinking:** The belief that positive thoughts and affirmations can manifest positive outcomes in one's life. This emphasis on the power of positive thinking is a common theme in New Age teachings.
- **Alternative healing:** The belief in the effectiveness of alternative healing modalities, such as acupuncture, reiki, and homeopathy. New Age practitioners often embrace these practices as complementary or alternative to traditional medicine.
- **Environmentalism:** The belief in the interconnectedness of all living things and the importance of preserving the planet. New Age teachings often emphasize the need for sustainable practices and respect for nature.

It is important to note that the New Age movement is not a monolithic entity. It contains a wide range of beliefs and practices. Some individuals may identify with only a few core themes, while others may embrace them all. The New Age movement constantly evolves, and new ideas and practices emerge.

While some New Age beliefs and practices may seem compatible with Christianity initially, fundamental differences set them apart. Here's a breakdown of the critical areas of divergence:

A few characteristics of the New Age Movement's viewpoints on God are listed.

The exact start date of the New Age is debated, but it's generally associated with the late 1960s and early 1970s. This period saw a convergence of various factors, including:
- **Astrological beliefs:** The transition from the Age of Pisces to the Age of Aquarius is believed to bring about a new era of spiritual enlightenment and consciousness.
- **Counterculture movement:** A widespread social and cultural movement that challenged traditional values and norms, emphasizing peace, love, and individual freedom.
- **Spiritual and mystical practices:** Increased interest in Eastern philosophies, meditation, yoga, and other spiritual disciplines.

While the New Age movement gained significant momentum in the 1970s, its roots can be traced back to earlier periods, with influences from Theosophy, Spiritualism, and other esoteric traditions.

New Age: God is often viewed as an impersonal cosmic force or energy that permeates all things. This concept differs from the Christian understanding of God as a personal, triune being (Father, Son, and Holy Spirit) separate from creation yet intimately involved.

Christianity: God is a personal, loving, and all-powerful creator who desires a relationship with humanity. This relationship is central to the Christian faith.

The viewpoint of the New Age Movement on Jesus Christ is stated as follows.

New Age: Jesus is often seen as a wise teacher, but not necessarily the Son of God or the unique Savior of humanity. He is usually placed alongside other spiritual leaders from different religions.

Christianity: Jesus is the central figure of the Christian faith. He is believed to be both fully human and fully divine. He is the Son of God, who came to earth to redeem humanity from sin and death.

The viewpoint of the New Age Movement on Salvation is stated as follows.

New Age: Salvation is often seen as a personal journey of self-discovery and enlightenment. It may involve practices like meditation, yoga, or positive thinking.

Christianity: Salvation is a gift from God, received through faith in Jesus Christ and his sacrificial death on the cross. It involves forgiveness of sins and eternal life.

The viewpoint of the New Age Movement on Authority is stated as follows.

New Age: Authority often rests with personal experiences, intuition, and subjective Truth. There is no single authority figure or sacred text.

Christianity: The Bible is the authoritative source of Truth and guidance for Christians. It reveals God's character, plan for salvation, and moral standards.

While some New Age practices may promote positive values like peace and love, the core beliefs and worldview often contradict the fundamental tenets of Christianity.

The New Age Movement is a New Spirituality. This breakdown lays out the deception. The lines of separation become blurred.

1. ☐ Jesus was not and is not the only Christ, nor is he God.
2. ☐ "God" is impersonal and cosmic, a God of energy forces.
3. ☐ Man is himself, God, for he consists of and is the creator of "the forces." The man already exercises the powers inherent in his divinity and only needs to awaken. (EVERYONE HAS A   SPIRITUAL GIFT)
4. ☐ The man should seek and accept spiritual instruction and direction directly from the spirit world. (CONSCIOUS ALTERING TECHNIQUES)
5. ☐ All religions and religious teachings lead to the same goal. All are equally of merit.
6. ☐ The "ancient wisdom" of Babylon, Egypt, and Greece—not the Bible—is the basis of all Truth.
7. ☐ Sin and evil do not exist. Peace and love are the ultimate realities. [30]

The New Age Movement teaches that SIN does not exist; therefore, humanity did not need a Savior. All he needs is greater enlightenment.

People also say, "I don't see anything wrong with that," or "That's your opinion."

"The New Age Kingdom will be! Says Matthew Fox, the heretical Catholic priest whose life is devoted to his New Age, nature worship ministry. FOX preaches that there is coming 'A NEW PENTECOST, A NEW CREATION, and A SPIRITUAL AWAKENING THAT ALL THE WORLD'S RELIGIONS MIGHT SHARE IN.'"

In a world seeking answers, an experience with God has been eliminated. Now, it is about personal viewpoint. The Roman Empire considered it essential to create Christianity to control the masses. In doing so, they set up church government, eliminating the God of the Old Testament.

For Christians, one significant fact was ignored.

Jesus was a Jew, and the New Testament didn't exist, so Jesus had to follow what is referred to as the Old Testament. I address the issues in this book in the Old Testament.

DO NOT need to debate the scriptures; we need to obey them.

The Christian Faith teaches that we are no longer under the Law but under Grace. This argument is made because the laws in the Old Testament were not comprehensive.

When the Hebrew Bible was written, some laws had no foundation, and scribes wrote whatever pleased the ruler.

The danger of women wearing pants in this generation is that many now wear tight-fitting pants, and this excites a man sexually. With the lack of modesty, men have the constant temptation to deal with, and women know what they are doing.

Unisex fashions and hair designs are available in shirts, pants, hairstyles, and watches. Men even carry purses. (Often, I don't know if I am speaking to a man or a woman when I go out in public.)

Fact "The New Age Movement" teaches that all must unify and that there must be no barriers. ALL MUST FORM A ONE-WORLD RELIGION. Their man of peace and unity will soon arrive to greet his people. That man of peace and harmony to them is the ANTICHRIST to the Christian world.

I must address the term Christ.

The word "Christ" comes from the Greek word "Christos," which means "anointed one." It is the Greek translation of the Hebrew word "Messiah," which means "anointed one." In ancient times, people were anointed with oil to signify their special status or appointment to a particular role.

In Christianity, "Christ" is a title given to Jesus, signifying that he is the anointed one of God, the Messiah prophesied in the Old Testament. This title emphasizes his unique role as the Savior of humanity.

It's important to note that if Jesus had been the Messiah or anointed, he would have never destroyed the Old Testament. Christians base their beliefs concerning Jesus on the Old Testament. Get rid of the Old Testament, and you won't have any prophecy that describes Jesus as the Messiah.

The world has been deceived, but we don't have to follow the blind.

Chapter 5

Games People Play

Some religious groups strongly oppose Television and Movies.

Psalms 101:1 NLT: A psalm of David. I will sing of your love and justice, LORD. I will praise you with songs.

Psalms 101:2 NLT: I will be careful to live a blameless life--when will you come to help me? I will lead a life of integrity in my own home.

Psalms 101:3 NLT: I will refuse to look at anything vile and vulgar. I hate all who deal crookedly; I will have nothing to do with them.

Psalms 101:4 NLT: I will reject perverse ideas and stay away from every evil.

Psalms 101:5 NLT: I will not tolerate people who slander their neighbors. I will not endure conceit and pride.

Psalms 101:6 NLT: I will search for faithful people to be my companions. Only those who are above reproach will be allowed to serve me.

Psalms 101:7 NLT: I will not allow deceivers to serve in my house, and liars will not stay in my presence.

Psalms 101:8 NLT: *<u>My daily task will be to ferret out the wicked and free the city of the LORD from their grip.</u>*

AMERICAN COLLEGE DICTIONARY

It tells us the words "amuse," "divert," and "entertain" mean to occupy the attention with something pleasant—that which amuses and dispels the lethargy of idleness or pleases the fancy. Divert implies turning the attention from serious thoughts or pursuits to something light, amusing, or lively. That which entertains usually does so because of a plan or program that engages and holds the attention.

Finally, we have entertainment that eliminates boredom and offers nothing but good, clean, wholesome programming. Is this shaping us into a better version of ourselves?

Now, our hours can be filled with adventure, suspense, and action.

With the world of technology at our fingertips through the remote control, we can travel to foreign countries, live in mansions, be in the executive board room of a large corporation, or make new friends by getting to know people on talk shows.

In the early stages of media development, Television, and movie theaters emerged as powerful tools in shaping cultural and spiritual perceptions. With the evolution of technology, video games and computer games have added another layer of complexity to this landscape. The introduction of Television into society was not a random occurrence; it was a well-coordinated effort aimed at influencing public consciousness and cultural narratives.

"TELEVISION ENCYCLOPEDIA"

In this history of Television, he states that the preparation for this invention began as early as 600 B.C. when static electricity was discovered.

Most of the other discoveries that brought Television about happened between 1600-1939.

APRIL 30TH, 1939: "RCA and NBC introduced television on April 30th, as a service to the public, at opening ceremonies of New York World's Fair, featuring President Roosevelt as first Chief Executive to be seen by fully developed television."[1]

Is it coincidental that April 30th is the second-highest satanic holiday? (Halloween is the first) The holiday is called Walpurgisnacht.

"THE DEVIL'S NOTEBOOK."
EVANGELISTS VS. THE NEW GOD:
It comes as no surprise that the televangelists are being cashiered on all fronts, either through scandal or absurdity. People are wising up about the Swaggerts and the Roberts and Bakkers only because it is time for them to be allowed to wise up. Why? Because the Christ-sellers were beginning to compete with the very god that they were employing: TV

In previous centuries, the Church was the great controller, dictating morality, stifling free expression, and posing as conservator of all great art and music. Today, Television dictates fashions, thoughts, attitudes, and objectives as once did the Church, using many of the same techniques but doing it so palatably [agreeable to the mind or feelings] that no one notices.

Instead of "sins" to keep people in line, we fear being judged unacceptable by our peers (by not wearing the right running shoes, drinking the right kind of beer, or wearing the wrong kind of deodorant) and fear-imposed insecurity concerning our own identities. Borrowing the Christian sole salvation concept, Television tells people that only through exposure to TV can the sins of alienation and ostracism be absolved.

We don't have to go out early Sunday mornings to get religion -- that was too much work. Now, all we have to do is click the remote control, and Church comes to us. [2]

Hebrews 10:23 NLT: Let us hold tightly without wavering to the hope we affirm, for God can be trusted to keep his promise.

Hebrews 10:24 NLT: Let us think of ways to motivate one another to acts of love and good works.

Hebrews 10:25 NLT: And let us not neglect our meeting together, as some people do, but encourage one another, especially now that the day of his return is drawing near.

We're intimate with Television's comforting presence from the moment we emerge from our mother's womb; indeed, TV is omnipresent, shadowing us more than the obsolete God shadowed Joan of Arc.

Television sets are in every home, restaurant, hotel room, and shopping mall—now they're even small enough to carry in your pocket like electronic rosaries. Television is an unquestioned part of everyday life. Kneeling before the cathode-ray God, we maintain the illusion of choice by flipping channels (chapters and verses) with our TV Guide concordance in hand. It doesn't matter what is flashing on the screen–all that's important is that the TV stays on.

When the Church based its mandate on the Holy Bible as the word of God Almighty, it brought out the doubters because their claim betrayed a glaring lack of logic. The Holy Fathers devised the necessity for 'faith' in hopes of covering up the inherent problems. But when TV masquerades as 'entertainment,' there's no room for doubt. No absurd premises are being advanced, so no one has any cause to resist.

Television still influences your life no matter how much of a free thinker you believe you are. To deny TV now would be as atheistic as Ingersoll denying the existence of God. Naturally, the televangelists had to be cut off - they were alienating the sheep from the shepherd. The ends are the same as they always have been. Sheep must be kept in line and encouraged to deposit money in the right places. But the televangelists became too greedy in invoking God, siphoning off too big a chunk of money for themselves.

That's why the present "religious war" isn't between any forces of "Good" and "Evil." It is being waged between the Media (the State) and Churches (Catholic and otherwise).

They are tying up millions of dollars of valuable property and assets. As Satanists, we can realize this early in the game.

It has never been enough for us to be atheistic. We have learned how to smash religious ignorance by beating them at their own game, using the Christians' own manufactured fears to destroy them. We can use TV as a potent propaganda machine. The stage is set for the infusion of true Satanic philosophy and potent (emotionally inspiring) music to accompany the inverted crosses and pentagrams. Instead of holding our rituals in chambers designed for a few dozen people, we are moving into auditoriums crowded with ecstatic Satanists thrusting their fists forward in the sign of the horns. As much "bad press" as the Church of Satan has received from the media over the past few years–Satanic child abuse, sacrifices, etc.–mention of The Satanic Bible only points people in our direction. Perhaps that's the plan, after all.

The key is to use Television and not be used by it. Munitions makers don't try the new stuff out on themselves. Do it if it takes turning your Television to the wall or throwing it out the window. We are adversaries to be reckoned with and must not be taken in by our infernal devices. We must allow stratification to develop so that a world for the vital and living can be established and maintained. [3]

SOME EVIDENCE OF A NEW SATANIC AGE, PART II:

In the Satanic Bible, I provided some examples of how modern Christianity was modifying itself to keep in step with diabolical advances. Now, it's time to recognize yet another manifestation.

Many of you have already read my writings identifying TV as the new God. There is a little thing I neglected to mention up until now - Television is the prominent mainstream infiltration of the New Satanic religion.

The birth of TV was a magical event foreshadowing its Satanic significance. The first commercial broadcast was aired on Walpurgisnacht on April 30th, 1939, at the New York World's Fair. Since then, TV's infiltration has been so gradual and complete that no one noticed.

People don't need to go to Church anymore; they get their morality plays on Television. What began modestly as rabbit ears on top of family TV sets are now satellite dishes and antennas pride entirely dominating the skyline, replacing crosses on top of churches. The TV set, or Satanic family altar, has grown more elaborate since the early 50s, from the tiny fuzzy screen to massive "entertainment centers" covering entire walls with several TV monitors. What started as an innocent respite from everyday life has become in itself a replacement for real life for millions, a major religion of the masses. [4]

Instead of obeying the holy bible, right or wrong, TV advertising now instructs what to buy and what not to buy. [5]

There is no way a person can escape religion as long as he is living in a religious environment. Situation comedies, dramatic series, and soap operas are broadcast day and night, seven days a week, to activate and sustain the lifestyles of the parishioners. In contrast, before, only fanatics practiced daily devotions. The masses committed only one day, Sunday, to the Christian God. As I've said before, the TV guide is the new concordance. Tabloids and news magazines supply the instructions for pious living. TV devotion has become so pervasive that even motion pictures are today presented in the same fast-paced–limited information style. [6]

Lavey states, "The couch potato is equivalent to the Bible reader who has the Good Book present at all times, in every room–ornate family bibles in the living room, one on his nightstand, one handy in the kitchen. The Couch Potato rarely strays out of TV range.

Next on the list is the casual Christian who watches regularly. Television nevertheless influences Christianity and cannot or will not entertain anything outside the parameters of media input. The small-time parishes, inhabited by local newscasters, are the "true believers." [7]

2 Timothy 3:1 NLT: <u>You should know this, Timothy, that in the last days there will be tough times.</u>

2 Timothy 3:2 NLT: <u>For people will love only themselves and their money. They will be boastful and proud, scoffing at God, disobedient to their parents, and ungrateful. They will consider nothing sacred.</u>

2 Timothy 3:3 NLT: <u>They will be unloving and unforgiving; they will slander others and have no self-control. They will be cruel and hate what is good.</u>

2 Timothy 3:4 NLT: <u>They will betray their friends, be reckless, be puffed up with pride, and love pleasure rather than God.</u>

2 Timothy 3:5 NLT: <u>They will act religiously, but they will reject the power that could make them godly. Stay away from people like that!</u>

SATURDAY MORNING MIND CONTROL:
"... Television is not entertainment to a child; it is a teacher. And oh, the lessons it teaches." [8]

Children learn from repetition, noise, and visuals. "Until a child is seven, he sees TV as reality." [9]

In 1948, there were 250,000 TV sets in the world. Today, there are more than 750 million. The price of a midsize car in 1940 was $1,000, and a TV set was $660. Now, you can buy a midsize car for about $14,000 and a TV set for under $100. Television provides access to more than 71 million homes in the United States. [10]

"Between 1949 and 1952, the number of TV sets in the U.S. jumped from 190,000 to more than 16 million." [11]

The two selling techniques that work best with children soon became apparent. Offer something for free; a child understands free. A child also responds to a commercial in which the product is shown to be popular with other children.

Thus, the advertising formula became pretty set:
*Advertise your product with a superhero.
*on a program featuring the superhero
*with lots of slam-bang action and color,
*offer something free,
*show happy kids with the product,
*Place your message in the correct hour or half-hour time slot,
*Above all, encourage the children to ask their mom or dad to buy the product the next time they visit the store! [12]

"Two other significant things happened in the mid-1980s. In 1985, 20.6 percent of U.S. homes had videocassette recorders. Two years later, the percentage was 44.1 percent, now well over 50 percent." [13]

TV is a business, and they are there to make the money. They are teaching violence to our children.

1954 17% prime-time networks, 1960 60% "Two-thirds of all major characters get involved in violent or aggressive actions." [14]

In 2024, the percentage of people who own a television will vary depending on the country and region.

However, TV ownership is very high in developed countries, often exceeding 90%. The percentage may be lower in developing countries but still significant in most urban areas.

People who watch a lot of violent TV behave more aggressively.

Eastern Religion is promoted numerous times daily.

The thought "it doesn't matter what you believe" is pushed daily, and if you take a stand and tell someone it does matter, you must be ready to be labeled "judgmental."

"Both Eastern religions and occult practices employ a variety of symbols, myths, and methods that often overlap." [15]

Spiritism is the oldest form of religion on earth. Virtually every religion today, other than Judaism and Christianity, originated in Babylon. The seven basic principles of spiritism are these:

1. There is a supreme father.
2. All men are equal brothers.
3. Life is a continuous existence.
4. Man follows an endless progression.
5. A person's walk along that path is their responsibility; communion with spirits can help.
6. There will be rewards someday for those who follow good.
7. Most spiritists choose Satan as their father and demons as their consulting spirits, and they believe the path of life is one of reincarnation.

Today, nearly 750,000 people are avowed spiritists in the U.S., about one-third of the world's known adherents. As of 1991, this has undoubtedly increased. [16]

"Hinduism ... is not the same religion as that founded five thousand years ago.... Hinduism seeks to include all religions in some oneness." [17]

"Hindus believe not in a single God but in the idea of gods in everything...." [18]

"The religion has given rise to TM (transcendental meditation), a spiritual form of yoga." [19]

Hinduism generally holds that anyone can become enlightened to the point of being a god and that reaching this State is something man is responsible for doing on his own. It allows the worship of a wide variety of deities." [20]

Zen Buddhism, also known as Zen, is derived from the Japanese branch of the Buddhist meditation school. Introduced in Japan and China in the seventh century, it teaches that life is filled with sorrow and suffering and that a person can move from sorrow to a state of nirvana (perfection) through reincarnation. [21]

The Eightfold Path, also known as the Noble Eightfold Path, is a set of eight practices that Buddhists believe lead to the cessation of suffering and enlightenment. It is the fourth of the Four Noble Truths taught by the Buddha.

The Eightfold-Path is divided into three categories:
- **Wisdom:**

Right View: Understanding the Four Noble Truths.

Right Intention: Avoiding thoughts of attachment, hatred, and harmful intent.
- **Ethical Conduct:**

Right Speech: Refraining from lying, divisive speech, harsh speech, and senseless speech.

Right Action: Refraining from physical misdeeds such as killing, stealing, and sexual misconduct.

Right Livelihood: Avoiding trades that directly or indirectly harm others.
- **Mental Discipline:**

Right Effort: Abandoning negative states of mind, preventing negative states from arising, and sustaining positive states.

Right Mindfulness: Awareness of body, feelings, thoughts, and phenomena.

Right Concentration: Single-mindedness and meditative absorption.

The Eightfold Path is a holistic and interconnected set of practices that should be engaged simultaneously. It is a lifelong journey that requires dedication and effort.

To follow this path, one calls on his spirit within, and that alone. An individual is responsible for his salvation; there is no such thing as sin because there are no absolute standards of holiness.

The New Age philosophy holds one central overriding belief: wholeness, unity, and peace. Many of its symbols, practices, and buzzwords are derived from fragmentation, and one might find or achieve oneness.

Friendship is essential to achieving unity and a one-world environment. All MUST be friends, and cooperation is repeated in the messages given to children. [22]

Today, social media has focused on obtaining more likes and friends, and young people are judged on the invisible. Even avatars are created with Artificial Intelligence, which will cause emotional trauma to those who are addicted to their media.

Visual conditioning is essential. Many symbols are used repeatedly, including all-seeing eyes, circles and triangles in various combinations, rays of light, rising suns, and crosses with diagonals placed against them.

The rainbow is foremost. New Agers believe each rainbow color represents a god responsible for a particular human personality activity or trait. From a Christian context, the rainbow symbolizes God's covenant power with man never again to destroy the world with a flood. To a New Ager, the rainbow is connected to building a bridge between humanity and Lucifer, the light bearer, from manhood to godhood]. To fly to this new unity, New Agers use the symbol of a Pegasus (winged horse) or the unicorn. [23]

The unicorn and the winged horse (Pegasus) are common neopagan symbols. They are derived from Greek and Roman mythology, where gods and goddesses generally rode them. Pegasus received his power to fly when he was fitted with a golden bridle. It was his job to take lightning bolts and thunder to Zeus.

The unicorn and Pegasus have appeared generously associated with the New Age Movement, also called the Golden Age, the Age of Aquarius, and the Eon of Horus.

The new world order can be ushered on the wings of innocence and gentleness.

The unicorn has been a famous symbol since medieval times and is believed to have magical and healing powers. It is a symbol of transformation, the idea that the unicorn, with a whole, unified, single horn, represents the creation of a holistic social order. Unicorns are frequently coupled with rainbows, a symbol discussed earlier. [24]

One can achieve wholeness or holism using yoga, music meditation, psychic healing, macrobiotics, dreams, biofeedback, reflexology, self-help visualization methods, mind control, TM, positive thinking, and hypnosis.

Each of these four religious orientations aims to achieve a new world order. Most seek some means of raising the individual's consciousness (demon possession). Many recognize or employ the value of such occult practices as Astrology, which studies the positions and movements of celestial bodies and their potential influence on human affairs. Fortune telling involves predicting future events, often through various methods such as tarot cards or palm reading. Ascended masters refer to spiritually enlightened beings who guide individuals on their paths.

The concept of 'the force' can relate to various spiritual and metaphysical beliefs about an underlying energy or power. Astral projection is experiencing an out-of-body journey, allowing the individual to explore different planes of existence. Numerology studies the mystical significance of numbers and their impact on human life.

Necromancy involves communicating with the dead, often for divination purposes. Parapsychology is the scientific study of phenomena outside traditional psychological explanations, such as telepathy or clairvoyance. The third eye is usually associated with heightened perception and intuition.

Tarot cards are divination tools that provide insight into situations and challenges. Ouija boards are used to communicate with spirits or to seek guidance from supernatural sources. Spirit guides are believed to be benevolent entities that offer assistance and protection.

Magic encompasses a wide range of practices aimed at harnessing supernatural forces. Levitation refers to rising or floating in the air, often associated with magical or mystical experiences. Telepathy is the purported ability to transmit thoughts directly from one mind to another.

Wizardry is using one's knowledge of occult sciences to achieve desired outcomes. Spiritism is the belief in the ability to communicate with spirits and the belief in their influence on the living. Clairvoyance is gaining information about an object, person, or event through extrasensory perception (E.S.P.).

Humanism always holds that man is capable of self-fulfillment, generating peace on earth, and conducting himself in proper ethical conduct solely by his efforts and without recourse to God. [25]

"Shamanism is the official term for practices where a spirit guide is consulted for wisdom. A belief in an unseen world of gods, demons, and human ancestral spirits characterizes it. The shaman's guardian spirits were considered to be the spirits of his ancestors. A shaman is a "priest who uses magic to cure the sick, divining the hidden, and controlling events." [26]

"Possession is also an occult phenomenon." [27]

Most New Agers are aware of the dangers present when practicing altered states of consciousness–demon possession. They boast of the experience.

Occultists generally view the following as the eight means by which a person might become fully realized as a medium, witch, or priestess:

1. The use of dance or ritualistic movement.
2. The use of wine, incense, drugs, or other chemical inducements that can cause the spirit to be released.
3. meditation and concentration, especially staring at mental images, whether imagined or real.
4. The use of language in rites, charms, spells, and runes.
5. Scourging.
6. Controlled breathing and other forms of physical control, such as lowering blood pressure or increasing blood flow.
7. The great rite, which is ceremonial sexual intercourse.
8. Achieving a state of trance or astral projection. [28]

MANY OF THESE APPEAR ON THE TELEVISION IN THE CHILDREN'S CARTOONS!

What should a parent do?

If you answer "yes" to any of the following questions, then ban the item regardless. If the item is in your house, remove it.
1. ☐ Anything with wizards, witches, or spirits (good or bad).
2. ☐ Are there demons, spirits, or familiars that help certain characters achieve their goals?
3. ☐ Does the item have occult symbols, such as pentagrams or goats' heads?
4. ☐ Does the item portray occult practices, such as seeing into the future, levitation, mind control, divination, communication with the dead, and so forth?
5. ☐ Are there any witchcraft or occult tools on the items? (Such as wearing amulets, holding wands or staffs with magical powers, or consulting books of spells)?

When choosing a toy or game for your children, read the product description. Watch for words about Magic, mysticism, enchantment, fantasy, fairies, angels, enlightenment, travel to a land, etc.

Symbolism is the most robust way that NAM (NEW AGE MOVEMENT) reaches our lives.

The history of video games is a fascinating journey that spans several decades, marked by groundbreaking innovations and cultural shifts. Here's a brief overview of its key milestones:

Early Beginnings (1950s-1960s):
- ☐ OXO (1952):1 Developed by A.S. Douglas, this tic-tac-toe game was one of the earliest examples of a computer-based video game.
- ☐ Tennis for Two (1958): Created by William Higinbotham, this simple tennis game was displayed on an oscilloscope and marked a significant step forward in interactive

Gaming.

The Golden Age of Arcades (1970s-1980s):

- **Pong (1972):** 4 Atari's Pong revolutionized the gaming industry, popularizing the concept of home video game consoles.
- **Space Invaders (1978):** This iconic arcade game introduced the shoot-'em-up genre and became a global phenomenon.
- **Pac-Man (1980):** 7 Developed by Namco, Pac-Man's maze-based gameplay and catchy music made it one of the most beloved arcade games ever.

The Home Console Era (1980s-Present):

- **Nintendo Entertainment System (NES) (1985):** Nintendo's NES brought console gaming back to life with iconic titles like Super Mario Bros. and The Legend of Zelda.
- **Sega Genesis (1989):** Sega's Genesis challenged Nintendo with its powerful hardware and innovative titles, such as Sonic the Hedgehog.
- **PlayStation (1994):** Sony's PlayStation revolutionized the gaming industry with its 3D graphics capabilities and a diverse library of games.
- **Xbox (2001):** Microsoft's Xbox entered the console market with online gaming capabilities and a focus on high-quality titles.

Modern Gaming (2010s-Present):

- **Mobile Gaming:** The rise of smartphones and tablets has led to a surge in mobile Gaming, with popular titles like Angry Birds and Pokémon GO.
- **Virtual and Augmented Reality:** VR and AR technologies push the boundaries of gaming experiences, offering immersive and interactive gameplay.
- **E-sports:** Competitive Gaming has become a significant industry, with professional gamers competing in tournaments worldwide.

The history of video games is a testament to human creativity and technological advancement. It continues to evolve, shaping popular culture and entertainment for generations.

Here are some of the most popular video games in recent years:

- **Minecraft:** A sandbox game where players can build and explore almost anything imaginable.
- **Fortnite:** A popular battle royale game with a unique building mechanic.
- **Grand Theft Auto V (GTA V):** A massive open-world game where players can explore the fictional city of Los Santos.

- **The Legend of Zelda:** Breath of the Wild: An open-world action-adventure game set in the world of Hyrule.
- **Red Dead Redemption 2:** A Western-themed action-adventure game set in the American frontier.
- **Overwatch:** A team-based first-person shooter game with colorful characters.
- **The Witcher 3:** Wild Hunt: An open-world RPG set in a dark fantasy world.
- **Animal Crossing: New Horizons:** A relaxing life simulation game where players can build their island paradise.
- **Super Smash Bros. Ultimate:** A fighting game featuring characters from various Nintendo franchises.
- **Elden Ring:** A challenging open-world RPG developed by FromSoftware.

The relationship between video games and behavior is a complex topic with ongoing research and debate.

Negative Influences:
- **Addiction:** Excessive gaming can lead to addiction, negatively impacting relationships, work, and health.
- **Aggressive Behavior:** While some studies have linked violent games to aggressive behavior, the evidence is mixed and complex.
- **Sedentary Lifestyle:** Prolonged gaming can contribute to a sedentary lifestyle, leading to health problems.

These are just a few of the many popular video games available today. The gaming industry constantly evolves, so watch for new and exciting titles!

This industry is raking in enormous profits at the cost of your family bonds, as a lack of communication and interaction leads to disconnection.

The video game industry is massive and lucrative, generating billions annually. In 2024, the global video game market was estimated at almost 455 billion U.S. dollars.

Here are some key sources of revenue for the video game industry:

1. Game Sales:

- **Physical Copies:** Sales of physical copies of games for consoles and PCs.
- **Digital Downloads:** Digital copies of games are sold through online stores like Steam, PlayStation Store, and Xbox Live.

2. Microtransactions:

- **In-game purchases:** Players can purchase virtual items, currencies, or other enhancements within the game.
- **Battle Passes:** Players can purchase premium passes that offer additional rewards and progression in games.
- **Loot Boxes:** Players can purchase randomized virtual items, often with a gambling-like mechanic.

3. Subscriptions:

- **Online Services:** Subscriptions to online gaming services like PlayStation Plus and Xbox Live, which offer access to multiplayer Gaming, exclusive content, and other benefits.
- **Game Subscriptions:** Subscriptions to game subscription services like Xbox Game Pass and PlayStation Plus Extra/Premium provide access to a library of games.

4. Advertising:

- **In-Game Ads:** Advertisements displayed within games, such as banners, video ads, or product placements.
- **Mobile Game Ads:** Mobile games often rely on advertising revenue, especially free-to-play games.

5. Licensing and Merchandising:

- **Licensing Fees:** Companies can license game characters, brands, and intellectual property for other products, such as toys, clothing, and movies.
- **Merchandise Sales:** Physical game merchandise, such as figurines, collectibles, and apparel.

The video game industry's revenue streams are diverse and constantly evolving. As technology advances and consumer preferences change, new revenue models may emerge, further driving the industry's growth.

The Influence of Video Games: A Double-Edged Sword

Video games have become an integral part of modern culture, influencing various aspects of society.

The average gamer spends about $76 monthly on their hobby, or $912 a year. This includes game purchases, subscriptions, and other gaming-related expenses.

However, this is just an average, and individual spending can vary significantly based on factors like:

- **Frequency of Gaming:** Casual gamers may spend less than those who play daily.
- **Platform Preference:** Console gamers might spend more on hardware and games than PC or mobile gamers.
- **Game Purchases:** The number and cost of games can substantially impact your overall spending, making it a key factor to consider.
- **Subscriptions:** Subscriptions to gaming services like PlayStation Plus or Xbox Live can add to monthly costs.
- **Microtransactions:** In-game purchases can significantly increase spending, especially for popular games with microtransaction systems.

It's important to note that these figures are not static. As the gaming industry evolves and new trends emerge, such as the rise of subscription services and the popularity of in-game purchases, these numbers can change.

Their impact can be positive and negative, depending on various factors such as the type of game, the player's age, and the amount of time spent playing.

The relationship between education and video games is complex, with potential benefits and drawbacks.

Potential Benefits of Video Games:

- **Cognitive Skills:** Many games can enhance problem-solving, decision-making, and strategic thinking skills.
- **Social Skills:** Multiplayer games can foster teamwork, communication, and cooperation.

- **Motivation:** Games can motivate players to achieve goals, persevere through challenges, and learn new skills.
- **Emotional Regulation:** Some games can help players manage stress and anxiety.

Potential Drawbacks:
- **Addiction:** Excessive gaming can lead to addiction, negatively impacting relationships, work, and health.
- **Aggressive Behavior:** While some studies have linked violent games to aggressive behavior, the evidence is mixed and complex.
- **Sedentary Lifestyle:** Prolonged gaming can contribute to a sedentary lifestyle, leading to health problems.

The main themes in video games are based on fantasy. Amulets and talismans invoke powers of darkness, introducing the player to multiple gods and goddesses. The occult pagan theme dominates minds.

The Role of Education:

<u>Education can play a crucial role in harnessing the positive potential of video games and mitigating their negative impacts. Here are some ways education can leverage video games:</u>
- **Educational Games:** Designing games that explicitly teach specific subjects or skills.
- **Gamification:** Incorporating game-like elements into traditional education to make learning more engaging.
- **Critical Thinking:** Teaching students to analyze game design, narrative, and social impact critically.
- **Digital Literacy:** Educating students about responsible gaming habits and online safety.

Conclusion:

Video games can be a powerful tool for education when used appropriately. By understanding their potential benefits and drawbacks, educators can leverage them to enhance learning experiences and foster positive development.

Positive Influences

- **Cognitive Benefits:** Many studies have shown that video games can enhance cognitive skills such as problem-solving, decision-making, and spatial reasoning.
- **Improved Reaction Time and Hand-Eye Coordination:** Action-oriented games can improve reflexes and hand-eye coordination.
- **Social Interaction:** Online multiplayer games can foster social connections and friendships, especially for those who may be socially isolated.
- **Stress Relief:** Gaming can be a relaxing and enjoyable way to unwind and reduce stress.
- **Educational Value:** Educational games can teach valuable skills, such as math, science, and history.

Negative Influences

- **Addiction:** Excessive Gaming can lead to addiction, negatively impacting mental health, relationships, and academic performance.
- **Physical Health Issues:** Prolonged Gaming can contribute to sedentary lifestyles, leading to obesity and other health problems.
- **Social Isolation:** Excessive Gaming can reduce social interaction and lead to feelings of loneliness and isolation.
- **Aggressive Behavior:** Some studies have linked violent video games to increased aggression, although the evidence is mixed and complex.
- **Sleep Disruptions:** Late-night Gaming can disrupt sleep patterns, leading to fatigue, irritability, and difficulty concentrating.

It's important to note that video game impact is highly individual and depends on various factors. Moderation is essential, and parents should encourage a balanced approach to Gaming, ensuring that it doesn't interfere with other important activities like school, work, and social interactions.

By understanding both the positive and negative aspects of video games, individuals can make informed choices about their gaming habits and maximize the benefits while minimizing the risks.

Would you like to know more about a specific aspect of video game influence, such as their impact on mental health or their role in education?

Some of the characters on the market that introduced the occult started years ago. Here are a few:

Winnie the Pooh, Bat Man, Muppets, Barney, Beauty & The Beast (enchantment), Lion King, Hook, Casper, Aladdin, Indian in the Cupboard, Free Willy, Snow White, Superman, Peter Pan, Pagemaster (Follow Me), Baby Bop, Jungle Book, Thumbelina, Wizard of Oz, Disney Talespins, Indiana Jones, Little Mermaid

Use this list to determine if the product promotes the occult.
1.☐Anything that has wizards, witches, or spirits (good or bad)
2.☐Are there demons, spirits, or familiars that help certain characters achieve their goals?
3.☐Does the item have occult symbols, such as pentagrams or goats' heads?
4.☐Does the item portray occult practices, such as seeing into the future, levitation, mind control, divination, communication with the dead, and so forth?
5.☐Are there any witchcraft or occult tools on the items? (Such as wearing amulets, holding wands or staffs with magical powers, or consulting books of spells)?

Below, you will see how occultic terms are introduced in advertisements. The list provided here shows some of the toys and games in 1994.

PRINCESS OF THE FLOWERS: (collection of dolls)
Create your enchanted garden. Unlock the Magic.
Every Princess of the Flower lives in a timeless place where wishes & dreams come true! It's an enchanted garden with a secret surprise inside each magical flower. With a turn of her unique key, the flower magically blossoms to reveal a beautiful princess in her fantasy world.

POLLY POCKET: Stardust fairy earrings, [On one doll, there is a third eye ornament]

BE YE HOLY

GARGOYLES HEROES: (demonic creatures) Kenner Toys 1995

Frozen in stone by day, flesh and blood winged warriors by night. Awaking after a thousand years, a band of powerful Gargoyles find themselves transported to a time and place not their own - New York City. Here, the misunderstood creatures battle modern-day barbarians and struggle to understand their strange New World Gargoyles the Legend begins.

GHOST BATTALION: Jasman Inc. 1995

"Rise. Rise that you may join my army of the dead." "Fight for me again; the world's riches will be yours." "What are your commands, oh vile one?"

X-MEN: Mojo

In the alternate dimension from which Mojo hails, TV has turned people into mindless video-enslaved people! Determined that his ratings would forever remain high, Mojo turned his super scientific arsenal against the X-men, recording the battles that followed for rebroadcast to his enslaved viewership.

Aladdin: Play as Aladdin through four magical stages of adventure! Call on Genie and the Magic Carpet for help! Rescue Jasmine from Jafar's evil clutches! Use your wishes wisely; you are only granted three!

Sonic Hedgehog promotes locating precious emeralds.

In **Lion King's "Circle of Friends,"** the entire message is one of voodoo.

Dr. Seuss's Stories teaches children about astral flight and the exercise of the imagination.

Crystal Baton - Magic Wand made by Slinky

Kaleidoscopes, holograms, and lava lamps are instruments used to teach meditation.

CASPER is the ghost of a twelve-year-old boy.

At least 72 divination methods have been introduced on Television, video, and computer games, along with other reinforcements to usher in the Antichrist.

COMPUTER GAMES:
WarCraft Orcs and Humans
Enter the world of WarCraft, a mystical land where evil Orcs and noble Humans battle for survival and domination. With ingenious weaponry and a powerful Magic arsenal, these two forces collide in a contest of cunning, intellect, and brute strength. Command many unique creatures, including demons, elementals, necromancers, archers, and spearmen.

Promoting the DOOM COMPANION is captivating, but its symbolism contradicts the core principles of faith.

DOOM COMPANION (1000 levels) New Levels: Dive into the extraordinary world of Doom modding, where the talented hackers have unleashed their most unsettling creations onto this expansive CD-ROM. Prepare yourself for an incredible journey through over 1,000 meticulously crafted levels, each brimming with new monsters, innovative weapons, captivating soundscapes, and surprises.

Set against the rich backdrop of Disc World, you will encounter a vibrant tapestry of characters, including wizards, fearsome dragons, courageous heroes, and skilled specialists, all ready to challenge your skills. However, tread carefully, as danger lurks around every corner. Yet, whimsical elements await amidst the perils—custard is splattered throughout various locales, adding a touch of absurdity to the adventure.

Disc World is a whimsical fantasy realm with an exceptionally low threshold for reality. This results in a constant interplay between the natural world and the fantastical elements that define it. This unique feature sets the tone for the game, making it a truly immersive experience. The very fabric of reality seems to unravel and morph with each passing moment as Disc World reshapes the ordinary into the extraordinary.

In addition to its thrilling gameplay, Disc World offers a unique artistic experience. It features photography, where tiny imps skillfully paint the visuals, and movies where those same nimble imps are caught in the act of painting at lightning speed. This artistic aspect adds value to the game, making it more than a gaming experience. The world is evolving, showcasing its second generation of computing technology—far superior to the outdated stone circles that once struggled to keep pace. Curiously, one of the images in the promotional material depicts a foreboding satanic circle adorned with a pentagram, hinting at the darker undercurrents lurking within this fantastical landscape. Prepare to embark on an unforgettable adventure where imagination reigns supreme!

KINGDOM BOOK ONE: The Far Reaches: An epic, Interactive Adventure the Whole Family will Enjoy. Long ago, in a land of five kingdoms, an amulet known as The Hand was shattered into five pieces and hidden throughout The Far Reaches. Dark Magic spread throughout the land, and the evil wizard, Torlok, began his reign of terror.

Now, the fate of the Five Kingdoms rests on Lathan, the last of the Argent Kings. To restore freedom, he must first recover the broken pieces of the amulet - but his journey is filled with many challenges. Danger and evil forces await as you guide Lathan on his quest for power and Magic.

Martial arts are based on weaponless fighting. They combine mental, physical, and spiritual energies to achieve various self-defense or paranormal feats of strength and control.

Their systematic use causes them to become a mystical religion to many participants.

A **role-playing game (RPG)** is a game where players assume the roles of characters in a fictional setting.

These characters can be anything from brave heroes to cunning villains, and they interact with each other and the game world to achieve their goals.

There are two main types of RPGs:

- **Tabletop RPGs:** These are played with dice, paper, and pencil, where players and a game master (GM) collaborate to create a story.3 Popular examples include Dungeons & Dragons and Pathfinder.
- **Video Game RPGs:** These are played on computers or consoles, where players control characters on a screen. Famous examples include The Elder Scrolls V: Skyrim, Final Fantasy VII, and Pokémon.

Both types of RPGs share some key features:

- **Character Creation:** Players create their characters with unique abilities and personalities.
- **Storytelling:** Players work together to create a story within the game world.
- **Decision Making:** Players make choices that affect the game's outcome.
- **Character Progression:** Characters gain experience and level up as they complete quests and challenges.

RPGs are popular because they offer players a unique and immersive experience. They allow players to explore different worlds, solve puzzles, and interact with various characters. RPGs can also be a great way to develop creativity, problem-solving skills, and teamwork.

Here are some of the most popular role-playing games (RPGs) across different platforms and genres:

Classic RPGs:

- **The Elder Scrolls V:** Skyrim: A vast open-world RPG set in the province of Skyrim.
- **The Witcher 3:** Wild Hunt: A critically acclaimed RPG set in a dark fantasy world.
- **Fallout: New Vegas:** A post-apocalyptic RPG set in the Mojave Wasteland.
- **Divinity:** Original Sin 2: A tactical RPG with deep character customization and co-op gameplay.
- **Disco Elysium:** A unique detective RPG focused on dialogue and character development.

Japanese RPGs (JRPGs):

- **Final Fantasy VII Remake:** A modern reimagining of the classic RPG.
- **Persona 5 Royal:** A stylish RPG with turn-based combat and social simulation ele-

ments.
- **NieR: Automata:** A thought-provoking action RPG with multiple endings and complex storytelling.
- **Tales of Arise:** A traditional JRPG with real-time combat and a captivating story.

Other Notable RPGs:
- **Baldur's Gate 3:** A highly anticipated RPG based on Dungeons & Dragons.
- **Elden Ring:** A challenging open-world RPG from FromSoftware.
- **Cyberpunk 2077:** A futuristic RPG set in the dystopian city of Night City.
- **Stardew Valley:** A relaxing farming RPG with a strong community focus.

This list is just a tiny sample of the RPGs available. With new titles being released regularly, there's always something new for RPG fans to explore.

Fantasy Role-Playing is dangerous. It involves the use of cards. Players cast spells, call up the dead, and become demonic characters.

Card Con: Collection of cards used in fantasy role-playing Jyhad, Spellfire Master the Magic, Advanced Dungeons & Dragons, Greyhawk, Dark Sun, Star Wars, Star Trek, Wyvern, Rage, Fights of Fantasy, Magic (the gathering), Illuminati (New World Order) along with Casper and many others.

A card con, or card convention, is an event dedicated to trading card games (TCGs) and other card-based hobbies. These events bring collectors, players, and sellers together to celebrate their shared passion.

Here is what you can typically expect at a card con:
- **Tournaments:** Competitive events for various TCGs like Magic: The Gathering, Yu-Gi-Oh!, Pokémon, etc.
- **Trading:** Opportunities to trade cards with other attendees.
- **Vendor Halls:** Booths where you can buy singles, booster packs, and other card-related merchandise.
- **Cosplay:** People dressed as characters from their favorite games or anime.
- **Gaming Areas:** Spaces for casual play and friendly matches.

- **Raffles and Giveaways:** Chances to win prizes, including rare cards and exclusive merchandise.
- **Artist Alley:** Where artists sell original artwork, prints, and custom cards.

Card cons are promoted: advertising states that they offer a great way to meet like-minded people, learn new strategies and expand your collection. They celebrate the vibrant and diverse community of card game enthusiasts.

2 Corinthians 10:1 NLT: <u>Now I, Paul, appeal to you with the gentleness and kindness of Christ--though I realize you think I am timid in person and bold only when I write from far away.</u>

2 Corinthians 10:2 NLT: <u>Well, I am begging you now so that when I come I won't have to be bold with those who think we act from human motives.</u>

2 Corinthians 10:3 NLT: <u>We are human, but we don't wage war as humans do.</u>

2 Corinthians 10:4 NLT: <u>We use God's mighty weapons, not worldly weapons, to knock down the strongholds of human reasoning and to destroy false arguments.</u>

2 Corinthians 10:5 NLT: <u>We destroy every proud obstacle that keeps people from knowing God. We capture their rebellious thoughts and teach them to obey Christ.</u>

2 Corinthians 10:6 NLT: <u>And after you have become fully obedient, we will punish everyone who remains disobedient.</u>

Romans 1:21 NLT: <u>Yes, they knew God, but they wouldn't worship him as God or even give him thanks. And they began to think up foolish ideas of what God was like. As a result, their minds became dark and confused.</u>

Romans 1:22 NLT: <u>Claiming to be wise, they instead became utter fools.</u>

Romans 1:23 NLT: <u>And instead of worshiping the glorious, ever-living God, they worshiped idols made to look like mere people and birds and animals and reptiles.</u>

Romans 1:24 NLT: <u>So God abandoned them to do whatever shameful things their hearts desired. As a result, they did vile and degrading things with each other's bodies.</u>

Romans 1:25 NLT: <u>They traded the truth about God for a lie. So they worshiped and served the things God created instead of the Creator himself, who is worthy of eternal praise! Amen.</u>

Romans 1:26 NLT: <u>That is why God abandoned them to their shameful desires. Even the women turned against the natural way to have sex and instead indulged in sex with each other.</u>

Romans 1:27 NLT: <u>And the men, instead of having normal sexual relations with women, burned with lust for each other. Men did shameful things with other men, and as a result of this sin, they suffered within themselves the penalty they deserved.</u>

Romans 1:28 NLT: <u>Since they thought it foolish to acknowledge God, he abandoned them to their foolish thinking and let them do things that should never be done.</u>

Romans 1:29 NLT: <u>Their lives became full of every kind of wickedness, sin, greed, hate, envy, murder, quarreling, deception, malicious behavior, and gossip.</u>

Romans 1:30 NLT: <u>They are backstabbers, haters of God, insolent, proud, and boastful. They invent new ways of sinning, and they disobey their parents.</u>

Romans 1:31 NLT: <u>They refuse to understand, break their promises, are heartless, and have no mercy.</u>

Romans 1:32 NLT: <u>They know God's justice requires that those who do these things deserve to die, yet they do them anyway. Worse yet, they encourage others to do them, too.</u>

In 2024, things on the earth are worse than in the days of Noah.

Genesis 6:5 NLT: <u>The LORD observed the extent of human wickedness on the earth, and he saw that everything they thought or imagined was consistently and totally evil.</u>

Genesis 6:6 NLT: <u>So the LORD was sorry he had ever made them and put them on the earth. It broke his heart.</u>

Genesis 6:7 NLT: <u>And the LORD said, "I will wipe this human race I have created from the face of the earth. Yes, and I will destroy every living thing--all the people, the large animals, the small animals that scurry along the ground, and even the birds of the sky. I am sorry I ever made them."</u>

Genesis 6:8 NLT: <u>But Noah found favor with the LORD.</u>

Genesis 6:9 NLT: <u>This is the account of Noah and his family. Noah was a righteous man, the only blameless person living on earth at the time, and he walked in close fellowship with God.</u>

Genesis 6:10 NLT: <u>Noah was the father of three sons: Shem, Ham, and Japheth.</u>

Genesis 6:11 NLT: <u>Now, God saw that the earth had become corrupt and was filled with violence.</u>

Genesis 6:12 NLT: God observed all this corruption in the world, for everyone on earth was corrupt.

Genesis 6:13 NLT: So God said to Noah, "I have decided to destroy all living creatures, for they have filled the earth with violence. Yes, I will wipe them all out along with the planet!

Philippians 4:8 NLT: And now, dear brothers and sisters, one final thing. Fix your thoughts on what is true, and honorable, and right, and pure, and lovely, and admirable. Think about things that are excellent and worthy of praise.

Philippians 4:9 NLT: Keep putting into practice all you learned and received from me--everything you heard from me and saw me doing. Then, the God of peace will be with you.

After reading this chapter, it is evident that wickedness surrounds us, and once evil things have become acceptable.

Chapter 6
Trendsetters

A Hair-Raising History: A Journey Through Hairstyles

Hair has always been a powerful tool of self-expression. From ancient to modern times, hairstyles have reflected cultural trends, social status, and personal identity. Let's take a brief journey through history to explore the fascinating evolution of hairstyles:

Ancient Times
• **Ancient Egypt:** Due to the hot climate, both men and women in ancient Egypt often shaved their heads. However, they adorned themselves with elaborate wigs of human hair, wool, or plant fibers. These wigs were usually styled in intricate braids and curls and decorated with gold, beads, or ribbons.
• **Ancient Greece:** Greek women favored long, flowing hair, often styled in loose waves or intricate updos. Hair was usually adorned with flowers, ribbons, or headbands. Men, on the other hand, typically kept their hair short.
• **Ancient Rome:** Roman women were known for their elaborate hairstyles, often involving intricate braids, curls, and updos. Hair was usually dyed, curled, and adorned with jewels and ornaments.

Medieval and Renaissance Periods
• **Medieval Europe:** During the Middle Ages, women's hair was often covered with veils or head coverings. When hair was visible, it was usually styled in simple braids or buns.
• **Renaissance Era:** The Renaissance saw a resurgence of interest in classical beauty, and

hairstyles became more elaborate. Women's hair was often curled and styled in intricate updos, adorned with jewels and feathers.

Modern Era
- 1920s: The roaring twenties brought a new era of short hair for women, popularized by figures like Coco Chanel and Louise Brooks. The bob haircut became iconic, symbolizing liberation and modernity.
- 1950s: The 1950s were characterized by glamorous, feminine hairstyles, such as the victory roll and the beehive.
- 1960s: The 1960s saw a shift towards more natural and effortless styles, with long, straight hair and the iconic pixie cut becoming popular.
- 1970s: The 1970s were a decade of experimentation, with various styles like the shag, the mullet, and Afro hairstyles gaining popularity.
- 1980s: The 1980s were known for big hair, with teased hairdos and perms being the norm.
- 1990s: The 90s brought a return to simpler styles, with grunge and minimalist looks dominating the scene.
- 2000s and Beyond: The 21st century has seen diverse hairstyles, from sleek and straight to curly and voluminous.

Hairstyles continue to evolve, reflecting each era's changing tastes and trends. Whether it's a classic bob or a bold, experimental style, hair remains a powerful tool of self-expression.

The early 2020s saw a diverse range of hairstyles influenced by both classic and modern trends.

Here are some of the most popular styles:
Women's Hairstyles:
- **The Polished Bob:** This classic cut made a comeback in 2020 with a modern twist. The polished bob was sleek, sharp, and often paired with a blunt fringe.
- **The Shaggy Mullet:** This playful and edgy style is characterized by longer back and shorter front layers.

- **The Textured Lob:** The long bob, or lob, remained a popular choice. In 2020, textured lobs with soft layers and waves were particularly trendy.
- **Natural Hair:** Embracing natural hair texture became more mainstream, with many women opting for styles like Afro puffs, twists, and braids.
- **Bold Hair Colors**: From vibrant hues like neon pink and electric blue to subtle balayage and ombre, bold hair colors were a major trend in 2020.

Men's Hairstyles:
- **The Classic Short Back and Sides:** This timeless style remained popular, often paired with a textured top or a slicked-back look.
- **The Modern Pompadour:** A modern take on a classic, the pompadour was often styled with a matte finish and a side part.
- **The Undercut:** This edgy style featured short, shaved sides and a longer top, often styled in a quiff or slicked back.
- **The Man Bun:** The man bun became popular for men with longer hair.

Remember, these are just a few of the many popular hairstyles of the early 2020s. Individual preferences and hair type played a significant role in determining the most suitable style for each person.

Hair has significant religious and cultural significance in various religions. Here are some examples:

Judaism:
- **Men:** Jewish men are generally expected to keep their hair short, though some Orthodox Jewish men grow peyos (sidelocks) and beards.
- **Women:** Married Jewish women are traditionally expected to cover their hair with a wig, scarf, or hat as a sign of modesty and respect.

Islam:
- **Women:** Many Muslim women cover their hair as a sign of modesty and respect. Can be done with a hijab, niqab, or burqa.
- **Men:** Many Muslim men grow beards as a sign of their faith and masculinity.

Christianity:
- **Women:** Some Christian denominations encourage women to cover their hair, particularly during prayer or worship services, as a sign of respect and modesty.

• **Men:** While there are no specific rules about hair length or style in Christianity, some denominations may have particular guidelines or traditions regarding hair.

Sikhism:

• **Men and Women:** Sikhs are not allowed to cut their hair as a sign of respect for God's creation. Both men and women typically wear turbans to cover their uncut hair.

Rastafarianism:

• **Men and Women:** Rastafarians do not cut their hair as a sign of their spiritual connection to God and nature. Dreadlocks are an everyday hairstyle among Rastafarians.

It's important to note that these are general guidelines, and specific practices may vary depending on individual beliefs and cultural traditions within each religion. Additionally, some people may follow these guidelines more strictly than others.

Hair has long held significant spiritual and symbolic meanings in various pagan traditions. It is often viewed as a conduit of energy, a connection to the divine, and a reflection of personal power.

Here are some of the ways hair has been viewed in pagan contexts:

Symbolism and Power

• **Connection to the Divine:** Hair is often considered a sacred part of the body, connecting individuals to the divine. Cutting hair can be seen as a symbolic act of offering or sacrifice.

• **Source of Power:** In many cultures, hair is believed to contain personal power or life force. Long hair, in particular, is often associated with wisdom, strength, and spiritual energy.

• **Protection:** Hair can be used in protective spells and rituals. Some people braid hair into charms or amulets for protection.

Ritual Practices

• **Hair Offerings:** Hair offerings have been used in various pagan rituals, such as leaving locks of hair at sacred sites or burning them as part of a spell.

• **Hair-Cutting Rituals:** Hair-cutting can be a significant ritual often associated with transitions, such as puberty, marriage, or death. It can symbolize letting go of the past and embracing a new phase of life.

Hair has long held significant spiritual and symbolic meanings in various pagan traditions. It is often viewed as a conduit of energy, a connection to the divine, and a reflection of personal power.

In contemporary Pagan practices, hair carries significant symbolic meaning. Many practitioners opt for natural hair, often avoiding chemical treatments and wearing it long. Some may perform hair-cutting rituals to signify considerable life events or transitions.

It's essential to understand that beliefs and practices surrounding hair vary widely among different Pagan traditions. Despite these variations, hair is often viewed as a powerful symbol, representing personal power, spiritual connection, and the cyclical nature of existence.

Moreover, hair has been closely linked to the symbolism and mythology of various deities across cultures, underscoring the universality of this symbolism. It is frequently associated with attributes such as power, beauty, fertility, and sometimes even danger.

Here are some examples of gods and goddesses connected to hair:
Norse Mythology:
- **Sif:** The goddess of the earth, known for her beautiful golden hair. Her hair was a symbol of fertility and prosperity.
- **Loki:** The trickster god who once cut off Sif's hair as a prank, leading to a severe conflict.

Greek Mythology:
- **Aphrodite:** The goddess of love and beauty, often depicted with flowing, golden hair. Her hair symbolized her allure and divine power.
- **Medusa:** A monstrous figure with snakes for hair, representing the dangers of unchecked power and the fear of female sexuality.

Hindu Mythology:
- **Parvati:** The goddess of love, fertility, and devotion, often depicted with long, flowing hair, symbolizing her divine beauty and power.

Egyptian Mythology:
- **Nefertiti:** The famous Egyptian queen is known for her elaborate hairstyles and wigs, symbolizing her status and power.

In many cultures, hair was considered a sacred part of the body and was often associated with spiritual power. It was frequently used in rituals and ceremonies and could be offered as a sacrifice to the gods.

The significance of hair in mythology reflects its deep cultural and spiritual meaning, highlighting its role in shaping human identity and belief systems.

Trendsetters in the Hair World

While it's challenging to pinpoint a single source for hair trends, a combination of factors and influencers shape the styles we see:

1. Celebrities and Influencers:
• **A-List Celebrities:** Rihanna, Zendaya, and Harry Styles often set trends with bold and experimental hairstyles.
• **Social Media Influencers:** Influencers on platforms like Instagram and TikTok showcase various styles, tutorials, and product recommendations, directly impacting consumer trends.

2. Fashion Designers and Stylists:
• **High-Fashion Shows:** Runway shows often feature avant-garde hairstyles that inspire future trends.
• **Celebrity Stylists:** These professionals collaborate with celebrities to create iconic looks replicated by the public.

3. Hair Salons and Stylists:
• **Salon Culture:** Hair salons and stylists play a crucial role in interpreting and adapting client trends.
• **Educators and Trend Forecasters:** Industry experts predict future trends and educate hairstylists on new techniques and products.

4. Cultural and Social Factors:
• **Music and Subcultures:** Music genres, such as punk, hip-hop, and K-pop, have significantly influenced hair trends.
• **Social Movements:** Social movements can impact hairstyles, as seen in the Afro-centric hairstyles of the Black Power movement.

Ultimately, it's the collective influence of these factors that shape hair trends. As technology and social media evolve, trendsetting accelerates, and individual expression and experimentation become increasingly important.

Trendsetting is the act of introducing new ideas, styles, or behaviors that influence the broader culture. Trendsetting individuals or groups are often called "trendsetters" or "influencers."

The Influence of Trendsetting on Our Daily Lives: Trendsetting significantly influences our everyday experiences, intricately shaping our preferences and actions in numerous ways. From the clothes we choose to wear and the gadgets we adopt to the food we eat and the entertainment we consume, trends act as guiding forces that reflect current social dynamics and cultural shifts. This phenomenon dictates our style and fosters a sense of belonging and identity as we navigate societal expectations and peer influences. Ultimately, trendsetting weaves itself into the fabric of our lives, impacting our decisions, shaping our tastes, and influencing how we connect with others in an ever-evolving landscape.

1. Fashion and Lifestyle:
- **Clothing and Accessories:** Trendsetters influence what we wear, from the latest fashion trends to everyday attire.
- **Beauty and Grooming:** They dictate popular hairstyles, makeup looks, and skincare routines.
- **Lifestyle Choices:** Trendsetters can influence our hobbies, interests, and even our choice of leisure activities.

2. Technology:
- **Gadgets and Devices:** Early adopters of new technologies, like smartphones and smartwatches, shape consumer preferences.
- **Apps and Software:** Trendsetting apps and software can revolutionize how we work, communicate, and entertain ourselves.

3. Social Behavior:
- **Social Norms:** Trendsetters can challenge traditional norms and introduce new social

behaviors, such as online activism or sustainable living.
- **Communication Styles:** They can influence how we communicate, from emojis to the rise of specific social media platforms.

4. Food and Culture:
- **Cuisine:** Trendsetters can introduce new cuisines, dietary trends, and food preferences.
- **Cultural Practices:** They can influence cultural practices, such as mindfulness, yoga, or specific forms of exercise.

Trendsetting plays a crucial role in shaping various facets of our world. By examining the underlying factors that drive trends and identifying the individuals who influence them, we can gain valuable insights into the ever-changing and dynamic landscape of culture and society. This constant evolution keeps us engaged and interested.

Key Players in Trendsetting: A Diverse Landscape

Understanding the dynamics within the group of trend contributors is not just important; it's crucial. It's the key to unlocking the secrets of contemporary societal changes.

Trends often reflect a blend of various factors. They can naturally emerge from a culture's collective consciousness. Ultimately, the individual consumer can accept or reject a trend.

Recently, there has been an increasing trend toward the incorporation of occult elements into mainstream culture, a phenomenon commonly referred to as "Occulture." This development has been influenced by a variety of factors, including:
- **Social Media:** Platforms like TikTok and Instagram have popularized occult-themed content, such as tarot readings, spellcasting, and witchcraft.
- **Pop Culture:** Movies, TV shows, and music often feature occult themes, making them more accessible to the mainstream audience.
- **Counterculture Movements:** The rise of counterculture movements has renewed interest in spirituality, mysticism, and the occult.

While many people are drawn to the aesthetics and symbolism of the occult, some may engage in practices that could be dangerous or exploitative.

When you see the signs of the occult, it's crucial to be mindful of the potential consequences of certain practices.

A trend is a general direction or pattern of change. It can refer to a variety of things, including:
• **Fashion and Culture:** A trend in fashion or culture is a particular style or behavior that becomes popular at a specific time. For example, the popularity of certain clothing styles, music genres, or social media platforms can be considered trends.
• **Technology:** Technological trends refer to developing and adopting new technologies. The increasing use of smartphones and artificial intelligence are examples of technological trends.
• **Economy:** Economic trends refer to the overall direction of economic indicators, such as GDP growth, inflation rates, and unemployment rates.
• **Social Behavior:** Social trends relate to changes in people's attitudes, behaviors, and values. For example, the growing awareness of climate change and social justice issues are social trends.

In essence, a trend is a pattern that emerges over time, reflecting changes in society, culture, technology, or the economy.

Beware, only some of what glitters and shines is gold.

The phrase "blind leading the blind" is a metaphor for a situation in which someone who lacks knowledge or understanding guides others who are equally ignorant. It implies a dangerous situation in which everyone involved will likely make mistakes or suffer negative consequences.

The phrase originates from the Bible, specifically in the following Scriptures.

<u>Matthew 15:14:</u>
<u>"Let them alone; they are blind guides. If the blind lead the blind, both will fall into a pit."</u>

This verse highlights the danger of following someone who is misguided or needs more knowledge. It suggests that relying on such a leader can lead to disastrous outcomes.

This metaphor is often used in everyday language to describe situations where people follow false or misleading information or leaders are incompetent or corrupt. It warns against mindlessly following others without critical thinking and discernment.

First, to completely understand why the Apostle Paul brought up the issue, let's examine the history behind the letters. What was the problem? Off to the Library, we hit the encyclopedias. Let's see where Corinth was and what was happening.

1 Corinthians 11:14-15 NKJV: <u>Does not even nature itself teach you that if a man has long hair, it is a dishonor to him? But if a woman has long hair, it is a glory to her, for her hair is given to her for a covering.</u>

THE NEW ENCYCLOPEDIA BRITANNICA 1992
"Corinthians, The Letter of Paul to the, also called THE EPISTLE OF ST. PAUL THE APOSTLE TO THE CORINTHIANS, either of two New Testament letters, or epistles, addressed from the Apostle Paul to the Christian community he had founded at Corinth, Greece." [1]

"The first letter, probably about A.D. 53-54 at Ephesus, Asia Minor, deals with problems that arose in the early years after Paul's initial missionary visit ©. A.D. 50-51) to Corinth and his establishment there of a Christian community." [2]

"Saddened by reports of dissension among the converts of various Apostles, Paul begins his letter with a reminder that all are 'servants of Christ and stewards of the mysteries of God' (4:1). Then while answering questions sent from Corinth, he addresses questions of immorality, marriage and celibacy, the conduct of women, the propriety of eating meat offered to idols, and the worthy reception of the Eucharist." [3]

"The Second Letter of Paul to the Corinthians (II Corinthians in the New Testament) was written from Macedonia in about A.D. 55. The letter, which may have been written after an actual visit by Paul to Corinth, refers to an upheaval among the Christians there, during which Paul had been insulted and his apostolic authority challenged. Because of this incident, Paul resolved not to go to Corinth again in person. Instead, he wrote an intervening letter (2:3-4; 7:8, 12), now lost, in which he told the Corinthians of his anguish and displeasure. Presumably, he sent a fellow worker, Titus, to deliver the letter to the community at Corinth. In the second letter, Paul expresses his joy at the news, just received from Titus, that the Corinthians had repented, that his (Paul's) authority among them had been reaffirmed and that the trouble-maker had been punished." [4]

Paganistic worship prevailed throughout humanity's history. Greece was one of the major countries involved in this activity. Greece began to worship Zeus as early as the 2nd millennium B.C., and this practice continued throughout its history. Greece was steeped in idolatry, so the Apostle Paul addressed idolatry by worshipping various gods and goddesses. Corinth was not exempt from this involvement.

"WORLD BOOK 1994"
RELIGION: "The Greeks believed that certain deities (gods & goddesses) watched over them and directed daily events. Families tried to please household deities with offerings and ceremonies. Each city-state honored one or more deities as protectors of the community and held annual festivals in their honor." [5]

GREEK DIVINITIES can be divided into several groups. The earliest group was the Titans, led by Cronus. The most influential group was the Olympians. Several ranks of divinities existed among the Olympians. The top rank consisted of six gods and six goddesses. The gods were Zeus, ruler of all divinities; Apollo, God of music, poetry, and purity; Ares, God of war; Hephaestus, blacksmith for the gods; Hermes, messenger for the gods; and Poseidon, God of earthquakes and the ocean. The goddesses were Athena, goddess of wisdom and war; Aphrodite, goddess of love; Artemis, twin sister of Apollo and goddess of hunting; Demeter, goddess of agriculture; Hera, sister and wife of Zeus; and Hestia, goddess of the hearth.

Three important gods became associated with the 12 Olympians. There was Hades, ruler of the underworld and brother of Zeus; Dionysus, God of wine and wild behavior; and Pan, God of the forest and pastures. [6]

Various cities looked to gods, goddesses, demigods, and other divinities for answers to their situations. For example, Athens looked to Athena as their protector. Ephesus became the center of the cult of Artemis, and the temple of Artemis in Ephesus was one of the Seven Wonders of the Ancient World.

We find that the gods and goddesses of Greek mythology held similar positions in Roman mythology. For example, each mythology had a goddess of love. The Greeks called her Aphrodite, while the Romans called her Venus. Another example is that the Greeks called the goddess of hunting and childbirth Artemis, while the Romans called her Diana.

"DICTIONARY OF GODS AND GODDESSES, DEVILS AND DEMONS"
ARTEMIS: Greek goddess of the hunt, who can be shown to share in the functions of several other divinities. At times, human sacrifice was used. As the goddess of birth, women sacrificed their hair to her as tokens of devotion. This goddess, remember, is the same as the Roman goddess Diana.

"MAN, MYTH & MAGIC' The Illustrated Encyclopedia of Mythology, Religion and the Unknown

DIANA was the same as Artemis; both were tomboy goddesses. In one of the stranger versions of the Kallisto story, She was a lesbian.

Commerce and trade with other nations promoted the gods and goddesses to be recognized elsewhere. The only time women had cut their hair was when worshipping pagan deities.

The hair was presented to the deities as worship and showed devotion. It represented submission to their favorite goddess for protection or other favors.

NATIONAL GEOGRAPHIC VOL. 141, NO. 6 JUNE 1972
About 700 B.C., the Anatolian populace began to build a series of shrines. The shrines were dedicated to an ancient mother goddess, an Anatolia godly worshiped deity. She much resembled and eventually assumed some of the attributes of the fertility goddess Ishtar, or Astarte, whose cult flourished throughout the Mesopotamian world. {Ishtar or Astarte are also goddesses active in the New Age}

In the wake of Alexander, who in the fourth century B.C. built a cultural bridge between Greece and Asia, this mother goddess, also known as Cybele in parts of Anatolia, entered the Greek pantheon in two forms: as Artemis, with a sanctuary at nearby Ephesus, and as Aphrodite, with a refuge at Aphrodisias.

From the first century B.C., when pagan Aphrodisians erected it, to the sixth century A.D., when Christian Aphrodisians converted it into a basilica, the grand marble Temple of Aphrodite ranked as the most critical structure in the city. Aphrodisias owed its great prosperity and probably its very existence to the widespread worship of this goddess.

"Glory of the city, the Temple of Aphrodite towers behind its blazing altar. Women enter to sacrifice their hair in annual mourning for the death of Aphrodite's lover, Adonis–a rite recreated by the artist from fragmentary ancient accounts. Later, Aphrodisiacs transformed the temple into a Christian basilica." [7]

Couldn't the Apostle Paul be telling the people, "We don't have the custom of the women cutting their hair and sacrificing it to the deities or pagan goddesses?"

It was a fact that women were to have long hair. Conversely, it should have been evident that men were to have short hair. Paul wrote, "Doth not even nature itself teach you that, if a man has long hair, it is a shame unto him?" The laws given to Moses outline that men were to look and act like men and women were to look and act like women.

"THE NEW SCHAFF - HERZOG ENCYCLOPEDIA of RELIGIOUS KNOWLEDGE"

Women never cut their hair (compare Jeremiah 7:29), and long hair was their most fantastic ornament (Cant. 4. 1; compare, I Corinthians 11.5; Cant. 7.5). To cut off a woman's hair and so expose her neck was the greatest contumely [insulting manifestation of contempt in words or actions; contemptuous or humiliating insult] (compare Jeremiah 7.29; I Corinthians 11.6). Naturally, much attention was given to the care of the hair, and the prophet's mockery shows that vain women in early times knew well how to twist curls and weave artistic braids (Isaiah 3.24; cf. Judith 16.8). Fragrant ointments played a significant part in the dressing of the head (Psalms 23.5 cxxxiii.2; Matthew 6.17; Luke 7.46). Unfortunately, no picture has been preserved to show the fashions of women's hair-dressing in ancient times; later, they copied the noble Roman dames. So Josephus notes the custom of sprinkling the hair with gold dust to make it brilliant (Ant. VIII., vi.3). [8]

Although no pictures show how women dressed their hair, we have proof that they did not cut it.

To support this statement, we read numerous books on fashion history, including how people dressed and wore their hair.

The two books we used were **20,000 YEARS OF FASHION**, The History of Costume and Personal Adornment by Francois Boucher, and **THE HISTORICAL ENCYCLOPEDIA OF COSTUMES** by Albert Racinet in 1988. Many examples and statements confirm that women have always worn their hair long.

When and why did American women start cutting their hair?

Before the 1850s, American women did not cut their hair.

The women's movement was responsible for the change in the 1850s (refer to "Should Women Wear Pants?"). The beginning of cutting hair and wearing pants took place at the same time. Women would automatically cut their hair when they put on their pants, which caused significant societal problems, making them unwilling to accept such behavior. Due to public rejection, many women quickly returned to the style of long hair and dresses. It was in the 1900s that we saw a change in the women's style of clothing and the cutting of hair. The women were attempting to be equal to or better than men.

Women in Hollywood and actresses on movie screens helped promote this idea.

BOW, CLARA GORDON (1905-1965):
A silent screen star who rocketed to success in the twenties, Clara Bow's film career was brief and mercurial, as befits the age of the FLAPPER. Her Brooklyn home and its resulting accent are often credited for her inability to transition to sound movies. Still, that home, and especially a dysfunctional mother, also caused emotional problems that plagued her all of her life." [9]

"Bow is remembered not only for her expressive ability in wordless stories but also because she represented a new screen sex symbol: a guileless girl-next-door type, in contrast to, for example, the sophistication of a Mae West. The 'Clara Bow haircut' was widely copied during her era, with its short, pixy style depicting the boyish, androgynous trends of the daring twenties." [10]

"**Flappers,** the term for the women in the 1920s who, by changes in dress and lifestyle, transformed forever the image of the women in the Western world. Motivated in part by their disillusioning and yet confidence-building experiences during World War I, "flappers" in both Britain and America were especially known for "bobbing" the long hair that women had historically worn piled heavily on their heads, cutting it instead into a short, straight style that required little care." [11]

The average person has between 90,000 and 150,000 hairs on their head. However, the exact number can vary depending on hair color and genetics.

For example:

- Blondes tend to have the most hair, around 150,000 strands.
- Redheads have the least, around 90,000 strands.
- Brunettes and black-haired individuals fall somewhere in between.

The Science of Hair: A Fascinating Journey

Hair, a seemingly simple part of our bodies, is a complex structure with a fascinating science behind it. Let's delve into some key facts:

Hair Structure

- **Keratin:** Hair primarily comprises Keratin, a tough protein that forms our nails, skin, and hooves.
- **Hair Follicle:** Hair grows from a tiny follicle embedded in the skin.
- **Hair Shaft:** The visible part of the hair, consisting of three layers: the cuticle, cortex, and medulla.

Hair Growth and Loss

- **Hair Growth Cycle:** Hair growth occurs in cycles, including phases of growth, rest, and shedding.
- **Hair Loss:** Hair loss is a common occurrence, and factors like genetics, hormones, and stress can influence hair loss patterns.

Hair Color and Texture

- **Melanin:** The pigment melanin determines hair color.7 Different types and amounts of melanin result in various hair colors, from black to blonde.
- **Hair Texture:** The shape of the hair follicle determines hair texture, ranging from straight to curly.

Hair Care Tips Based on Science

- **Gentle Cleansing:** Avoid harsh shampoos that can strip hair of its natural oils.
- **Conditioning:** Use a conditioner to hydrate and protect the hair shaft.
- **Heat Protection:** Use heat protectant products before using hot styling tools.
- **Healthy Diet:** A balanced diet of protein, vitamins, and minerals promotes healthy hair growth.
- **Regular Trims:** Regular trims can help prevent split ends and maintain healthy hair.

By understanding the science behind hair, we can make informed choices about hair care and styling. Remember, healthy hair reflects overall well-being, so take care of it, and it will reward you with its beauty and vitality.

Baldness generally occurs only in men. Although women may have thinning hair, they do not typically go bald.

Hair grows approximately half an inch a month or six to seven inches yearly. The maximum length that hair grows, on average, is 2 feet. Fifty to eighty hairs fall out daily and are replaced with at least that many. On average, the hair on your head is about three years old. Your hair and nails are made of the same substance, Keratin.

Many factors influence hair growth, including age, diet, general health, and skin condition. In hot weather, hair sheds, and in cold weather, extra hair grows.

The sex glands regulate the development of adult hair. The male sex hormone promotes the development of the beard and the body hair while hampering the growth of the head hair.

The action of the female hormone reacts just the opposite. Cutting the hair does not promote growth.

The Lord designed the system in which hair grows. Isn't it unique that only the hair on our heads grows to a certain length?

Whoever answered the question, "How long is long? " By responding, "As long as the Lord lets your hair grow," stated the absolute truth.

Tradition is a system of beliefs or behaviors passed down within a group or society, often with symbolic meaning or special significance. These practices and beliefs originate in the past and are handed down through generations.

Critical characteristics of tradition:
- **Historical Significance:** Traditions often have roots in the past, connecting us to our ancestors and cultural heritage.
- **Cultural Identity:** They contribute to a sense of belonging and shared identity within

a community or group.
- **Symbolic Meaning:** Traditions can symbolize essential values, beliefs, or life stages.
- **Oral or Written Transmission:** Traditions can be passed down orally (stories, songs, folklore) or through written texts (religious scriptures, historical records).

Examples of traditions include:
- **Religious practices:** Rituals, ceremonies, and beliefs associated with specific religions.
- **Cultural festivals:** Celebratory events with specific customs, foods, and decorations.
- **Family customs:** Traditions specific to families, such as holiday celebrations or naming practices.
- **Social customs:** Greetings, manners, and etiquette.
- **Cultural artifacts:** Traditional clothing, music, dance, and art forms.

Traditions can evolve but often retain their essence and symbolic meaning. They are vital in shaping our culture, values, and sense of community.

Some of the traditions in which we participate are the following: New Year's, Valentine's Day, Easter, Mother's Day, Memorial Day, Father's Day, Fourth of July, Labor Day, Thanksgiving, Christmas, etc. Originate in occult or pagan worship of other gods.

Let's look at the word TRADITION: The handing down of statements, beliefs, legends, customs, etc., from generation to generation, esp. by word of mouth or practice. Theology. a. (among the Jews) an unwritten body of laws and doctrines, or any of them, held to have been received from Moses and handed down orally from generation to generation. b. (among Christians) a body of teachings, or any one of them, held to have been delivered by Christ and His apostles but not committed to writing. Law. Act of handing over something to another, esp. in a formal legal manner; delivery; transfer.

The Bible, particularly the New Testament, contains several passages that critique traditions that deviate from God's Word or hinder spiritual growth. Here are some key verses:

Matthew 15:2 NKJV: "Why do Your disciples transgress the tradition of the elders? For they do not wash their hands when they eat bread."

Matthew 15:3 NKJV: He answered and said to them, "Why do you also transgress the commandment of God because of your tradition?

Matthew 15:6 NKJV: 'then he need not honor his father or mother.' Thus you have made the commandment of God of no effect by your tradition.

Mark 7:3 NKJV: For the Pharisees and all the Jews do not eat unless they wash [their] hands in a special way, holding the tradition of the elders.

Mark 7:5 NKJV: Then the Pharisees and scribes asked Him, "Why do Your disciples not walk according to the tradition of the elders, but eat bread with unwashed hands?"

Mark 7:8 NKJV: "For laying aside the commandment of God, you hold the tradition of men--the washing of pitchers and cups, and many other such things you do."

Mark 7:9 NKJV: He said to them, "[All too] well you reject the commandment of God, that you may keep your tradition.

Mark 7:13 NKJV: "making the word of God of no effect through your tradition which you have handed down. And many such things you do."

Colossians 2:8 NKJV: Beware lest anyone cheat you through philosophy and empty deceit, according to the tradition of men, according to the basic principles of the world, and not according to Christ.

It's crucial to approach traditions discerningly, ensuring they align with biblical principles and promote genuine faith.

2 Chronicles 7:11 NKJV: Thus Solomon finished the house of the LORD and the king's house; and Solomon successfully accomplished all that came into his heart to make in the house of the LORD and in his own house.

2 Chronicles 7:12 NKJV: Then the LORD appeared to Solomon by night, and said to him: "I have heard your prayer, and have chosen this place for Myself as a house of sacrifice.

2 Chronicles 7:13 NKJV: "When I shut up heaven and there is no rain, or command the locusts to devour the land, or send pestilence among My people,

2 Chronicles 7:14 NKJV: "if My people who are called by My name will humble themselves, and pray and seek My face, and turn from their wicked ways, then I will hear from heaven, and will forgive their sin and heal their land.

2 Chronicles 7:15 NKJV: "Now My eyes will be open and My ears attentive to prayer [made] in this place.

2 Chronicles 7:16 NKJV: "For now I have chosen and sanctified this house, that My name may be there forever; and My eyes and My heart will be there perpetually.

2 Chronicles 7:17 NKJV: "As for you, if you walk before Me as your father David walked, and do according to all that I have commanded you, and if you keep My statutes and My judgments,

2 Chronicles 7:18 NKJV: "then I will establish the throne of your kingdom, as I covenanted with David your father, saying, 'You shall not fail [to have] a man as ruler in Israel.'

2 Chronicles 7:19 NKJV: "But if you turn away and forsake My statutes and My commandments which I have set before you, and go and serve other gods, and worship them,

2 Chronicles 7:20 NKJV: <u>"then I will uproot them from My land which I have given them; and this house which I have sanctified for My name I will cast out of My sight, and will make it a proverb and a byword among all peoples.</u>

2 Chronicles 7:21 NKJV: <u>"And [as for] this house, which is exalted, everyone who passes by it will be astonished and say, 'Why has the LORD done thus to this land and this house?'</u>

2 Chronicles 7:22 NKJV: <u>"Then they will answer, 'Because they forsook the LORD God of their fathers, who brought them out of the land of Egypt, and embraced other gods, and worshiped them and served them; therefore He has brought all this calamity on them.'</u>

Chapter 7
Social Media

Pride is a complex emotion that can be both positive and negative.

Here's a breakdown of the different aspects of Pride:
Positive Pride
- **Self-respect:** A healthy Pride in one's accomplishments and abilities.
- **Group pride:** Belonging and connection to a community or group.
- **National Pride:** Loyalty and patriotism towards one's country.

Negative Pride
- **Hubris:** Excessive Pride or arrogance, often leading to downfall. •Vanity: Excessive concern with one's appearance or achievements.
- **Prejudice:** Belief in the superiority of one's group.

Pride can be a motivating force that drives us to achieve our goals and connect with others. However, it's essential to maintain a healthy balance and avoid excessive Pride, which can lead to negative consequences.

While Pride and confidence may seem similar, they are distinct emotions with different implications. Here's a breakdown of the key differences:
Pride:
- **Focus on self:** Pride often centers around achievements, abilities, or status.
- **Self-aggrandizement:** It can involve boasting, bragging, or seeking validation from others.

- **Negative connotations:** Excessive Pride can lead to arrogance, haughtiness, and a sense of superiority.
- **External validation:** Prideful individuals may rely on external factors like praise or recognition to feel good about themselves.

Confidence:
- **Focus on abilities:** Confidence is rooted in a belief in one's capabilities and potential.
- **Self-assurance:** It involves a sense of self-worth and self-efficacy.
- **Positive connotations:** Confidence is generally seen as a positive trait that can lead to success and happiness.
- **Internal validation:** Confident individuals draw strength from their beliefs and accomplishments rather than seeking external validation.

At its core, Pride can be a double-edged sword; it can become a destructive force that obstructs personal growth and negatively impacts relationships with others. In contrast, confidence emerges as a positive and empowering attribute that inspires individuals to pursue their goals with determination and resilience.

So, is there a difference between Pride and confidence? While the two concepts may appear similar, they are fundamentally different, each built on its unique foundation. Confidence is rooted in self-assurance and belief in one's abilities, whereas Pride often stems from an inflated sense of self-worth and can lead to detrimental behaviors. Understanding these distinctions is crucial for personal development and fostering healthy interactions.

Confidence:
- **Grounded in evidence:** Confidence is often rooted in past experiences, knowledge, or skills.
- **Tangible outcomes:** It's based on what we can see, measure, or control.
- **Self-reliance:** Confidence often involves believing in one's ability to overcome challenges.

Faith:
- **Beyond evidence:** Faith often involves belief in something that cannot be proven or verified.
- **Intangible outcomes:** It's based on hope, trust, and a belief in something greater than

oneself.
- **Divine reliance:** Faith often involves trusting a higher power or a spiritual force.

In essence:
- Confidence is a belief in oneself, often grounded in tangible experiences.
- Faith is believing in something beyond oneself, often without tangible evidence.

While both can be powerful forces, they operate on different principles and serve various purposes.

I have never been confident in my abilities, for I realize that everything I do depends entirely on trusting God.

Below is Scripture telling how God looks at Pride.

2 Chronicles 32:26 NLT: <u>Then Hezekiah humbled himself and repented of his Pride, as did the people of Jerusalem. So the LORD's anger did not fall on them during Hezekiah's lifetime.</u>

Job 35:12 NLT: <u>And when they cry out, God does not answer because of their Pride.</u>

Job 36:9 NLT: <u>he shows them the reason. He shows them their sins of Pride.</u>

Psalms 59:12 NLT: <u>Because of the sinful things they say, because of the evil that is on their lips, let them be captured by their Pride, their curses, and their lies.</u>

Psalms 73:6 NLT: <u>They wear Pride like a jeweled necklace and clothe themselves with cruelty.</u>

Psalms 73:8 NLT: <u>They scoff and speak only evil; in their Pride they seek to crush others.</u>

Psalms 101:5 NLT: I will not tolerate people who slander their neighbors. I will not endure conceit and Pride.

Proverbs 6:3 NLT: follow my advice and save yourself, for you have placed yourself at your friend's mercy. Now swallow your Pride; go and beg to have your name erased.

Proverbs 8:13 NLT: All who fear the LORD will hate evil. Therefore, I hate Pride and arrogance, corruption and perverse speech.

Proverbs 11:2 NLT: Pride leads to disgrace, but with humility comes wisdom.

Proverbs 13:10 NLT: Pride leads to conflict; those who take advice are wise.

Proverbs 16:18 NLT: Pride goes before destruction, and haughtiness before a fall.

Proverbs 29:23 NLT: Pride ends in humiliation, while humility brings honor.

Isaiah 2:11 NLT: Human pride will be brought down, and human arrogance will be humbled. Only the LORD will be exalted on that day of judgment.

Isaiah 2:17 NLT: Human Pride will be humbled, and human arrogance will be brought down. Only the LORD will be exalted on that day of judgment.

Isaiah 13:11 NLT: "I, the LORD, will punish the world for its evil and the wicked for their sin. I will crush the arrogance of the proud and humble the Pride of the mighty.

For over 55 years, I have trusted God, for I know how he loves those who serve and honor him. Every task I have set out to do has been taken on by asking God to open my understanding and show me how to accomplish a project. Over the years, I have learned that God has always opened my knowledge if I step out on faith after I feel strongly impressed.

When you celebrate your accomplishments, it is easy to let Pride take over your actions, which can lead to narcissism.

Narcissism is a personality trait defined by an intense focus on oneself and one's needs, frequently to the detriment of others. Individuals diagnosed with narcissistic personality disorder (NPD) display a variety of behaviors that reflect this preoccupation. These behaviors can include a lack of empathy, a need for admiration, and a tendency to exploit interpersonal relationships for personal gain. Understanding these traits is essential in recognizing and addressing the impact of NPD on both the individual and those around them.

- **Grandiosity:** An inflated sense of self-importance and a belief in their uniqueness.
- **Need for admiration:** A constant craving for attention and validation.
- **Lack of empathy:** Difficulty understanding or caring about the feelings of others.
- **Entitlement:** A sense of superiority and the expectation of special treatment.
- **Exploit:** A tendency to take advantage of others for personal gain.

Here is Scripture that provides a list of things that God hates.

Mark 7:20 NLT: <u>And then he added, "It is what comes from inside that defiles you.</u>

Mark 7:21 NLT: <u>For from within, out of a person's heart, come evil thoughts, sexual immorality, theft, murder,</u>

Mark 7:22 NLT: <u>adultery, greed, wickedness, deceit, lustful desires, envy, slander, Pride, and foolishness.</u>

Mark 7:23 NLT: <u>All these vile things come from within; they are what defile you."</u>

On Friday, September 22, 1995, the Dallas Morning News reported that Oxford University had rewritten the New Testament and Psalms, so it would now be Politically Correct.

What has happened to America? How did we go from being a God-fearing nation to one who has very little respect for Him or His Word?

Every aspect of Christianity is being challenged. In a desperate attempt to draw people back to church, Christian Leaders have compromised, unknowingly incorporating into their worship services paganistic practices.

Why the transformation? Society felt that the various restrictions placed upon people caused hypocrisy, so traditional Christianity began its compromise.

First, they sought for greater spiritual enlightenment.

They used meditation, yoga, music, and aroma therapy methods. They were oblivious that the enemy had tricked them.

Satan has conditioned people to accept anything new and "recommended by professionals."

Sin has destroyed family units. People have become self-centered and egotistical, disregarding others, including family members. Drugs, alcohol, and immoral sexual practices have become Satan's surest tools of destruction. Feelings of hopelessness grip the hearts of loved parents, husbands, wives, and children who are searching for answers to help those who Satan is tormenting.

When society started turning to Psychology versus turning to God, the world went off the scale in their actions, creating a god-like attitude.

Let's take a closer look at forgiveness.

Forgiveness is a complex and multifaceted concept that can be approached from various perspectives. Here's a breakdown of its key aspects:

What is Forgiveness?

- **A Choice:** Forgiveness is a conscious decision to release resentment and anger towards someone who has harmed you. It's not about condoning their actions or forgetting what happened, but rather about letting go of the negative emotions that hold you back.
- **A Process:** Forgiveness is often a journey, not a single event. It may involve stages like acknowledging the hurt, understanding the reasons behind the harm (if possible), and finally, choosing to release the pain.
- **A Gift to Yourself:** While forgiveness can benefit the person who harmed you, it primarily benefits the forgiver. It can increase peace of mind, reduce stress, and improve well-being.

It is essential to understand that you do not have control over another person's actions and are not accountable for their harmful behavior. Your responsibility lies in how you treat others and maintaining your well-being. If you find yourself in a situation where someone has harmed you—whether emotionally, physically, sexually, or spiritually—it is crucial to establish clear boundaries to protect yourself.

Recognizing red flags in relationships is essential for your safety and peace of mind. If you want to live a life aligned with your faith, consider reading the Bible for guidance. Finding a place to worship and enjoy joyous fellowship can significantly enhance your spiritual journey and support network.

Beware: Not everyone who attends a church or professes to love God is faithful. The best place for demonic spirits to hide is within a church. You have to evaluate a person's actions and compare their conversations to see if their actions agree.

If they exhibit behavior contrary to Scripture, that is a red flag. Below is the best way to test who an individual is serving.

Galatians 5:19-21 NLT: ***When you follow the desires of your sinful nature, the results are very clear: sexual immorality, impurity, lustful pleasures, idola-***

try, sorcery, hostility, quarreling, jealousy, outbursts of anger, selfish ambition, dissension, division, envy, drunkenness, wild parties, and other sins like these. Let me tell you again, as I have before, that anyone living that sort of life will not inherit the Kingdom of God.

Read the scriptures above. Anyone participating in any of this does not serve God but serves self. Do not become friends with these people.

When you see words in scriptures that you don't understand, look them up online.

How you deal with those sinning against God is listed below.

Galatians 5:22-23 NLT: *But the Holy Spirit produces this kind of fruit in our lives: love, joy, peace, patience, kindness, goodness, faithfulness, gentleness, and self-control. There is no law against these things!*

Remember that you can not be around those who are rebellious against God.

The next question you will ask is how I will ever win people to God if I don't interact with them. When in a social situation, take every opportunity to share what God has done for you; that is your testimony.

It would be best to protect your spiritual being; you don't do that by being friends with the world.

James 4:4 NLT: *You adulterers! Don't you realize that friendship with the world makes you an enemy of God? I say it again: If you want to be a friend of the world, you make yourself an enemy of God.*

James 4:17 NLT: *Remember, it is sin to know what you ought to do and then not do it.*

When individuals serve God, they want to please Him. Watching and listening is the best way to find out if you are attending a place of worship that pleases God.

Spiritual leaders are required to reflect authentic leadership without compromise.

How do I know if I am attending the proper place of worship?

Start with the basics. The Ten Commandments were not ten suggestions. If the place you are going for your spiritual instructions doesn't follow these, you are in the wrong place.

What did Jesus teach and live by? God gave us the commandments listed below, which relate to our relationship with God.

Jesus never declared he was God to do this would be that he would be stoned. Go back and read the New Testament closely. Jesus knew who God was. Without question, he obeyed the commandments.

Exodus 20:1-11 NLT: *__Then God gave the people all these instructions: "I am the LORD your God, who rescued you from the land of Egypt, the place of your slavery. "You must not have any other god but me. "You must not make for yourself an idol of any kind or an image of anything in the heavens or on the earth or in the sea. You must not bow down to them or worship them, for I, the LORD your God, am a jealous God who will not tolerate your affection for any other gods. I lay the sins of the parents upon their children; the entire family is affected--even children in the third and fourth generations of those who reject me. But I lavish unfailing love for a thousand generations on those who love me and obey my commands. "You must not misuse the name of the LORD your God. The LORD will not let you go unpunished if you misuse his name. "Remember to observe the Sabbath day by keeping it holy. You have six days each week for your ordinary work, but the seventh day is a Sabbath day of rest dedicated to the LORD your God. On that day, no one in your household may do any work. This includes you, your sons and daughters, your male and female servants, your__* *livestock, and any foreigners living among you. For in six days the LORD made the heavens, the earth, the sea, and everything in them; but on the seventh day he rested. That is why the LORD blessed the Sabbath day and set it apart as holy.*

The debate over what day to worship has gone on for centuries. If you declare yourself to be a Christian, then that means Christ-like. And what day did Jesus go to the synagogue or temple?

Initially, the Sabbath was from Friday sundown until Saturday sundown.

Look at a calendar: the first day of the week is Sunday.

The Catholic Church changed the Sabbath. To find out this information, search "When did the Catholic Church change the Sabbath?"

This list says nothing about forgiveness, so let's look deeper into that topic.

*Galatians 5:22-23 NLT: **But the Holy Spirit produces this kind of fruit in our lives: love, joy, peace, patience, kindness, goodness, faithfulness, gentleness, and self-control. There is no law against these things!***

Where did we get the idea that we had the power to forgive sins? The Catholic leadership implemented this idea, but it also shows up in society through various psychologies. Taking a closer look at forgiveness, we see the following.

The Benefits of Forgiveness
- **Emotional Healing:** Forgiveness can help you release negative emotions like anger, resentment, and bitterness, allowing you to heal and move forward.
- **Improved Relationships:** While it doesn't necessarily mean reconciling with the person who hurt you, forgiveness can improve your relationships with others by fostering empathy and understanding.
- **Enhanced Mental Health:** Studies have shown that forgiveness can reduce symptoms of depression, anxiety, and stress.

- **Spiritual Growth:** Many people find that forgiveness is a spiritual practice that can deepen their connection to themselves and others.

How to Forgive

1. **Acknowledge the Hurt:** The first step is acknowledging the pain and hurt you've experienced. Don't try to minimize or deny your feelings.
2. **Understand the Offender:** If possible, understand the reasons behind the person's actions. If substance abuse is present, then their actions stem from demon possession. However, if the person has gone through challenging times and strikes out at you, try to understand what they have experienced. This can help you develop empathy and compassion.
3. **Avoid self-blame and negative talk**.
4. **Let Go of Resentment:** Make a conscious decision to release resentment and anger toward the person who hurt you and not to go around them.
5. **Focus on the Future:** Instead of dwelling on the past, focus on the future and the positive aspects of your life.

Curious to find out where the grips of sin began, I felt that it was necessary to research the origins of mental health. My research took me to the thresholds of psychology.

This breakdown of the centuries will help lay out when theories began.

The 19th century spanned the years 1801 to 1900, the 20th century covers the years 1901 to 2000, and the 21st century began on January 1, 2001, and will end on December 31, 2100.

Psychology began its journey towards popularity in the late 19th century. During this time, psychology emerged as a distinct scientific discipline, thanks to the pioneering work of Wilhelm Wundt, who established the first psychology laboratory in 1879.

However, it was in the early 20th century that psychology truly gained widespread recognition.

With his exploration of the unconscious mind and psychoanalysis, Sigmund Freud's ideas captivated the public's imagination. His theories, though controversial, sparked intense debates and discussions, bringing psychology to the forefront of public consciousness.

Influential figures like Carl Jung, known for his analytical psychology, and B.F. Skinner, recognized for behaviorism, significantly contributed to psychology's rising popularity. Their innovative research and theories challenged traditional ideas about human behavior and mental processes.

B.F. Skinner was a highly influential American psychologist, behaviorist, author, inventor, and social philosopher. He is best known for his work on operant conditioning, a type of learning in which behaviors are shaped and maintained by their consequences.

Here are some critical points about B.F. Skinner:
- **Operant Conditioning:** Skinner's research focused on how behavior can be modified through reinforcement and punishment. He used experimental chambers, often called "Skinner boxes," to study animal behavior.
- **Radical Behaviorism:** Skinner's philosophy, known as radical behaviorism, emphasized the importance of environmental factors in shaping behavior. He argued that free will is an illusion and that external stimuli and reinforcement determine human behavior.
- **Contributions to Psychology:** Skinner's work has significantly impacted psychology, education, and therapy. His ideas have been applied in various fields, including behavior modification, education, and organizational behavior.
- **Notable Works:** Skinner authored numerous books, including "The Behavior of Organisms," "Walden Two," and "Beyond Freedom and Dignity."
- **Legacy:** B.F. Skinner is considered one of the most influential psychologists of the 20th century. His research and theories continue to shape our understanding of human behavior and learning.

In the mid-20th century, the cognitive revolution took place, shifting the focus of psychology from behavior to mental processes like perception, memory, and problem-solving. This cognitive perspective resonated with the public's increasing interest in understanding the mind's inner workings.

Today, psychology is an integral part of modern society. It has applications in various fields, including education, healthcare, business, and law. People increasingly seek psychological help to address personal challenges and improve their well-being. The popularity of psychology continues to grow, as it offers valuable insights into the complexities of human behavior and the human mind.

While psychology has its roots in the 19th century, its rise to popularity was indeed marked in the early 20th century, and its influence continues to shape our understanding of ourselves and the world around us.

Sigmund Freud, Carl Jung, and Carl R. Rogers were instrumental in the dawning of Modern Psychology.

Sigmund Freud was an Austrian neurologist and the founder of psychoanalysis. He is often considered the "father of modern psychology." Freud's theories revolutionized how we think about and treat mental health conditions.
   Here are some of his key contributions:
- **Psychoanalysis:** This clinical method involves dialogue between a patient and a psychoanalyst to explore unconscious thoughts and feelings.
- **The Unconscious:** Freud believed that our unconscious mind plays a significant role in our behavior and experiences.
- **Dream Analysis:** He interpreted dreams as symbolic expressions of unconscious desires and conflicts.
- **Psychosexual Stages:** Freud proposed a theory of psychosexual development, suggesting that childhood experiences shape adult personality.

While some of Freud's theories have been challenged and revised over time, his work remains influential in psychology and has had a lasting impact on our understanding of the human mind.

Carl Gustav Jung was a Swiss psychiatrist and psychoanalyst who founded the school of analytical psychology. Along with Sigmund Freud, he is considered one of the most influential thinkers of the 20th century.

Here are some of his critical contributions to psychology:

• **Collective unconscious:** Jung proposed the concept of the collective unconscious, a universal reservoir of archetypes shared by all humanity. Archetypes are universal symbols and patterns that influence our thoughts, feelings, and behaviors.

• **Introversion and extroversion:** Jung developed the concept of personality types, including introversion and extroversion. He believed that these personality traits are fundamental to understanding human behavior.

• **Individuation:** Jung believed that the goal of psychological development is individuation, a process of self-discovery and integration of the conscious and unconscious aspects of the psyche.

Jung's work has significantly impacted various fields, including psychology, literature, art, and philosophy. His ideas continue to be studied and applied today.

Carl R. Rogers was a renowned American psychologist who played a pivotal role in developing humanistic psychology. He is best known for his person-centered approach to therapy, which emphasizes the importance of empathy, unconditional positive regard, and genuineness in the therapeutic relationship.

Rogers's critical contributions to psychology include:

• **Person-Centered Therapy:** This therapeutic approach focuses on the client's experiences and feelings, with the therapist providing a supportive and non-judgmental environment.

• **Unconditional Positive Regard:** This concept emphasizes accepting and valuing clients without conditions.

• **Empathy:** Rogers believed that therapists should strive to understand clients' feelings and perspectives from their point of view.

• **Genuineness:** Authentic and sincere communication is essential for building client trust and rapport.

Rogers's humanistic approach has significantly impacted psychotherapy and counseling practices. His emphasis on the individual's potential for growth and self-actualization continues to inspire and influence contemporary psychological thought.

Edward Bernays, often called the "father of public relations," pioneered public relations and propaganda. He was a nephew of Sigmund Freud and drew heavily on his uncle's theories of psychology to manipulate public opinion.

Here are some critical points about Edward Bernays:

- **Pioneering Public Relations:** He developed innovative techniques to influence public perception and consumer behavior.
- **The Engineering of Consent:** Bernays coined this term to describe the process of manipulating public opinion using psychological principles.
- **Influential Campaigns:** He was involved in numerous high-profile campaigns, including promoting cigarettes to women as a symbol of liberation and encouraging Americans to eat more bacon.
- **Controversial Legacy:** While his contributions to the field of public relations are undeniable, his methods have also been criticized for their manipulative nature and potential to undermine democratic values.

Bernays's work has had a lasting impact on how we consume information and make decisions. His legacy continues to be debated, as his techniques are still used today, often without public awareness.

Psychology has played a significant role in bringing about this tremendous spiritual transformation (degradation).

But how could a profession set on helping humanity be used to introduce the One World Religion, also known as "The New World Order?"

For many years, I strongly desired to attend college and study psychology to equip myself better to help hurt people. I was introduced to the subject by reading books from the library and other books I purchased from Christian psychologists, such as Dr. James

Dobson. Infrequently, I have spoken with counselors about different ways to help those hurting.

I went to a local junior college and took a test, preparing to continue my education. Then it happened, and I took time to pray about my decision.

While in a church service, the Lord spoke to me. He said, "Trust me." I responded, "I do." Then He said, "No, you don't," or you would not attend college. God wasn't saying that all college was terrible but that what I chose to do had nothing to do with helping people.

A few more things were spoken to my heart that night, and by the time it was over, I had decided not to go.

Little did I know that three years later, God would reveal why my career choice had been canceled.

This information is not being given to destroy those who are not privileged to have it when selecting their careers. If you know a secular or Christian Psychologist, show them the love of God by sharing this vital information with them in love—not condemnation.

We hear the term "self-esteem" almost daily. Preachers preach about self-esteem; newspapers, schools, and businesses promote the concept. Corporations teach self-esteem seminars to encourage creativity and productivity. These seminars use channeling, meditation, and breathing techniques to reduce stress.

Many of the techniques are occultic in origin and stem from Eastern Religion in one form or another.

Psychology is not Biblical. It is based upon ideas that oppose the Word of God.

"NEW AGE ENCYCLOPEDIA, First Edition: An Overview of the New Age Movement"

Parapsychology: Equally important, psychology nurtured psychical research and its laboratory-oriented branch, parapsychology. As questionable as these two sub-disciplines' accomplishments within psychology have been, they supplied a unique seedbed from which new speculations could regularly emerge. The admission of the Para Psychological Association into membership in the American Academy for the Advancement of Science served to further the process of legitimization of 'scientific' metaphysical thought.

The latest appropriation of psychology - a necessary step in forming the New Age–followed the emergence of humanistic psychology and its derivative, transpersonal psychology. Humanistic psychology projected a much more positive approach to religious phenomena. In contrast, transpersonal psychology further concentrated on "religious" states of mind and utilized the spiritual disciplines (from meditation to magic) most advocated by metaphysical practitioners as primary research tools. In their attempts to isolate the effects of various spiritual disciplines, the transpersonal psychologists accomplished one unplanned but essential task. Their methodologies separated particular practices (such as meditation or yoga techniques) from the religious ideological context in which they had been developed and justified their free movement from one to another. For example, one could practice Zen meditation without becoming a Buddhist or chant mantras without becoming a Hindu. Concurrently, transpersonal psychology lent scientific respectability to a new language of consciousness, creativity, and personal transformation to explain the observed changes accompanying the use of the spiritual techniques, a language eagerly adopted by the emerging movement in the 1970s." [1]

Parapsychology is a specialized branch of psychology that rigorously explores psychic phenomena, including clairvoyance and extrasensory perception.

PSYCHOLOGY: The science of mind, or mental states and processes; the science of human nature; the science of human and animal behavior.

People seek psychological counseling for a variety of reasons, often related to emotional, mental, or behavioral challenges. Some common reasons include:
Emotional Distress:
- **Anxiety and Stress:** Excessive worry, fear, or nervousness.

- **Depression:** Persistent sadness, hopelessness, and loss of interest.
- **Grief and Loss:** Difficulty coping with the death of a loved one or other significant losses.

Relationship Issues:
- **Marital or Partner Problems:** Conflict, communication difficulties, or infidelity.
- **Family Conflict:** Disagreements, tension, or dysfunction within family relationships.
- **Social Anxiety:** Difficulty interacting with others or fear of social situations.

Life Transitions:
- **Job Loss or Career Changes:** Stress and uncertainty related to career transitions.
- **Moving or Relocation:** Adapting to new environments and cultures.
- **Retirement:** Adjusting to a new phase of life.

Trauma and Abuse:
- **Past Trauma:** Difficulty coping with past traumatic experiences, such as abuse or neglect.
- **PTSD:** Symptoms of post-traumatic stress disorder, including flashbacks, nightmares, and hypervigilance.

Substance Abuse:
- **Addiction:** Struggling with alcohol or drug addiction.
- **Codependency:** Difficulty setting boundaries and maintaining healthy relationships.

Other Reasons:
- **Self-Improvement:** Seeking personal growth and development.
- **Decision-Making:** Difficulty making essential life choices.
- **Low Self-Esteem:** Negative self-perception and lack of confidence.

Psychology encourages individuals to override right and wrong and accept evil. In this chapter, I have pointed out what type of people to avoid. If every person reading this book looks deeply into their life, they will discover that those who have wronged them are not following the principles of God.

Psychology keeps you in the past, while your focus needs to be on your current life. If you don't go around evil people, your life will not be complicated.

Philippians 3:13 NLT: *<u>No, dear brothers and sisters, I have not achieved it, but I focus on this one thing: Forgetting the past and looking forward to what lies ahead,</u>*

The number of people who see a psychologist varies by country and year. However, there has been a significant increase in the number of people seeking psychological help in recent years.

Here are some statistics to give you an idea:
In the US:
In 2023, around 59.2 million adults received treatment or counseling for their mental health within the past year.
About 30% of American adults have seen a therapist since 2020.

In the UK:
Around one person in eight (12.1%) receives mental health treatment.

It's important to note that these numbers are estimates, and the number of people seeking psychological help may be higher. Additionally, the stigma surrounding mental health is decreasing, and more people are recognizing the importance of seeking professional help.

Treatment for Mental Health conditions can vary depending on the specific diagnosis and severity of symptoms. However, combining therapy and medication is often the most effective approach.

Psychotherapy, or talk therapy, involves regular sessions with a mental health professional to discuss thoughts, feelings, and behaviors.

Different types of therapy include:
- **Cognitive-behavioral therapy (CBT):** focuses on identifying and changing negative thought patterns and behaviors.
- **Psychodynamic Therapy:** This explores past experiences and unconscious conflicts to

understand current symptoms.
- **Humanistic Therapy:** This emphasizes personal growth and self-actualization.
- **Family Therapy:** This focuses on improving communication and relationships within families.

Medication plays a significant role in managing symptoms of various mental health conditions, including depression, anxiety, and bipolar disorder. It's important to note, however, that some prescribed medications may contribute to mental confusion and carry a risk of addiction.

Alternative treatments may provide additional support in addition to medication and therapy. Some of these therapies may have unconventional associations, including beliefs related to spiritual influences. Exploring various treatment options can be beneficial in finding the most effective approach for individual mental health needs.

- Alternative Therapies: Yoga, meditation, and acupuncture may help reduce stress and improve overall well-being. The dangers of the occult are apparent if these techniques are researched.
- Brain Stimulation Therapies: Techniques such as electroconvulsive therapy (ECT) and transcranial magnetic stimulation (TMS) may be used in severe cases of depression or other conditions.

The information below is dated at least 20-plus years ago.

"THE FACTS ON SELF-ESTEEM, PSYCHOLOGY, AND THE RECOVERY MOVEMENT" by John Ankerberg & John Weldon

In 1957, 10 million people sought psychological counseling, 20 million in 1983, and 40 million in 1995. It has become a 30-billion-dollar industry.

Unfortunately, there isn't a single, definitive number for the exact total of psychotherapists and paraprofessionals in the USA. However, we can provide some estimates based on available data:

Psychotherapists:
Therapy 4 the People: Estimated a total of 530,000 therapists in 2022, including:
106,000 clinical psychologists
250,000 clinical social workers
120,000 licensed counselors
50,000 marriage and family therapists

Paraprofessionals:
- **Mental Health Technicians:** The exact number is difficult to pinpoint, but it's a significant number, especially in hospitals, clinics, and residential treatment facilities.
- **Peer Support Specialists:** The number varies widely depending on state and local programs.
- **Community Health Workers:** Again, the number is variable, but it's a growing field, particularly in underserved communities.

Recognizing that these figures are estimates is essential, and the actual numbers could be even greater. An important question: if these therapies were effective, why do so many individuals still seek help from mental health professionals?

Additionally, the number of mental health professionals is constantly changing due to factors such as retirement, new graduates, and changes in healthcare policies.

If you want more specific information, consider consulting with professional organizations like the American Psychological Association (APA) or the American Counseling Association (ACA). They may have more detailed data on the number of licensed professionals in specific states or regions.

Every aspect of our lives has been affected, including psychology in industry, science, medicine, schools, church, business, and family life.

Religious organizations have been compelled to include professional counselors on staff to avoid legal issues. In the years gone by, people handled their problems seeking wise, godly counsel. Still, instead of having individuals who deeply care about providing an individual with wise counsel, spiritual leadership avoids interaction at all costs for fear of being accused of causing more mental health issues.

The presuppositions that provide the general framework within which most psychology is practiced include the following nine ideas:

Naturalism: is the doctrine that all religious truth is derived from studying natural processes, not revelation. This doctrine states that natural religion is sufficient for salvation. Naturalist psychologists Thus reject the idea of a Creator God.

Materialism: The philosophical theory regards matter and its motions as constituting the universe and all phenomena, including those of the mind, due to material agencies. This idea supports self-interest and teaches that this is the first law of life. One should be devoted to material rather than spiritual objects, needs, and considerations. "This means that the materialist psychologist believes that what we see is what we get and that God is completely irrelevant, for by definition, there is no spiritual dimension to reality. In this view, man has no spiritual nature, and personality is reduced to brain function." [2]

Reductionism: "...Assumes that all personhood and all human behavior can be explained by reducing them to the physiological, biological, and chemical processes accompanying human activity. Again, such a psychologist sees no spiritual or even necessary moral dimension to reality." [3]

Determinism: The doctrine that neither outer events nor human choices are uncaused but are the results of antecedent conditions, physical or psychological. "This ultimately has a determinist psychologist rejecting human freedom, dignity, and responsibility because people do not personally decide their actions; other causes predestine their behavior." [4]

Evolution: "...Attempts to provide the original explanation for human personality's existence, complexity and nature. It, too, is based on a materialistic worldview: Because all things have evolved naturalistically from simpler forms, God becomes irrelevant, and

Scripture becomes false for teaching such things as a supernatural creation or absolute morality. (According to Time (August 15, 1994), the field of evolutionary psychology has now concluded that men are destined to be sexual predators and adulterers because evolutionary forces are concerned only with "ruthless genetic self-interest" - driving men to sow their seeds far and wide irrespective of their marriage vows.)" [5]

Empiricism: "...Assumes that a person can know something only through the senses and scientific method. Thus, the empiricist psychologist believes that anything that cannot be proven to exist as sensory data does not exist. Of course, this includes such things as God, mind, angels, demons, and the human spirit." [6]

Relativism: The theory of knowledge or ethics holds that judgment criteria are relative, varying with the individual, time, and circumstance. "... Assumes that everything is relative and nothing is absolute. There are no absolute standards of right or wrong or good or evil. Under this view, psychologists can choose their personal moral views - and psychotherapy, whether speculative, bizarre, or even harmful. When applied to modern psychology and counseling, relativism opens the door for the serious abuse of patients among pragmatic and experimentally-oriented psychotherapists." [7]

Secular Humanism: "Is to varying degrees a logical result of all the above and assumes that man is the most important thing in the universe. Since no God exists, man is a God who does whatever he pleases. The humanist psychologist can promote the exaltation of self, justifying perceived interests with absolute sanction." [8]

Occultism: "...A logical corollary of Humanism constitutes certain beliefs and practices that undermine the Christian worldview in many ways. While it accepts a spiritual dimension to reality, the spirituality exalted is that of the devil, not God's, and so everything spiritual is perverted into the opposite of what God intends. The occult psychologist can become a kind of sorcerer, dispensing occult knowledge and power as psychological enlightenment to unsuspecting laypeople who initially only wanted help in solving their everyday problems. The irony is that occult practices are inherently dangerous both psychologically and spiritually, and to offer them as therapy is nothing less than a form of malpractice." [9]

What about the CHRISTIAN PSYCHOLOGIST?

A Christian psychologist is a mental health professional who integrates Christian faith and biblical principles into their therapeutic practice. They believe that faith can play a significant role in healing and personal growth.

Here are some critical aspects of Christian psychology:

- **Integration of Faith and Psychology:** Christian psychologists strive to integrate their understanding of the Bible and Christian theology with psychological theories and techniques.
- **Biblical Counseling:** They often incorporate biblical principles and teachings into their counseling sessions, using Scripture to provide guidance and comfort.
- **Holistic Approach:** Christian psychologists often take a holistic approach to mental health, considering their clients' spiritual, emotional, and physical well-being.
- **Focus on Spiritual Growth:** They may emphasize spiritual growth and development as part of the healing process.

It's important to note that while Christian psychologists incorporate faith into their practice, they are still trained mental health professionals who can provide evidence-based therapies.

They may profess that they can help individuals address a wide range of mental health concerns, including anxiety, depression, relationship issues, and trauma. Then why does therapy consist of years of continuous counseling?

While this article sounds impressive, let's look deeper into the individuals considered the fathers of psychology. Where did they get their theories?

How can a person study the therapies and techniques involved with psychology that are totally "Anti-Christian" and, upon completion of their college education, disregard all that they have been taught?

The following is a brief background on psychology.

"In psychoanalysis or depth psychology, we have founders Sigmund Freud 1856-1939 and Carl Jung 1875-1961. Freud hated religion, especially the Christian religion; he actively sought to destroy people's faith in the Christian God. " [10]

"Freud considered religious beliefs illusions and referred to religion as 'the obsessional neurosis of humanity.' " [11]

Like Freud, occult psychologist Carl Jung resented historic Christianity and especially its God. For him, it was only a myth sought after by neurotics. 'All neurotics seek the religious,' he said, and all talk to God is mythological. Therefore, the 'Protestant theologian' should abandon his ... alleged knowledge of God through faith and admit to the layman that he is mythologizing. Jung saw Biblical Christianity as hollow, irrelevant, and harmful...." [12]

Carl Rogers was the most important leader of humanistic psychology. Raised as a Christian, "...he became a leader in humanism and eventually turned to mysticism, spiritism, and the occult—which he hoped would be incorporated into our educational system." [13]

"Psychology today is increasingly accepting the occult -- so much so that a large text would be needed to do justice to this topic. In 1988, psychologist Gary Collins wrote, 'There is evidence that occult practices have been accepted by a large and perhaps growing number of psychological professionals.' "Indeed, their numbers are growing daily. Jungian, humanistic, shamanistic, transpersonal, Hindu, Buddhist, and fringe or esoteric psychologies, as well as parapsychology, are now fusing psychology and the occult as a means of very powerfully changing people." [14]

Discussing the integration of psychology and biblical teachings raises essential questions. Many Christians advocate for a synthesis of these two fields, seeking to find common ground. However, it is necessary to note that psychology does not have strong biblical support as it is understood today. Scripture consistently emphasizes that true strength and healing are found in the Lord. The Bible provides comprehensive guidance for addressing life's challenges. Relying on counseling grounded in psychological theories may imply that Adonai alone cannot adequately heal a troubled heart, contrasting with the biblical perspective on divine sufficiency.

Above all, the New Age is preoccupied with the deep self, the Higher Self, the True Self, and so on. New Agers, in principle, reject the very thought of negative self-image, self-talk, or self-esteem; such would be psychological sacrilege, blasphemy against "the God within." One idea is that "God is everything," anything we do has "an inner action of divinity," and that if we remember that, we will learn to love ourselves.

For the New Age, poor self-esteem and an unenlightened self-image are seen as the root causes of all our problems. **Self-esteem ignores humanity's fundamental problem—"SIN."**

In his book, Groothuis states, "Pride is the overestimation of ourselves as independent and the underestimation of our dependence on God." [15]

All of the self-talk and self-esteem in the world will not cover sin. One of our most significant societal problems is the feeling that we must be catered to. We hold grudges and demand that the Lord move when we snap our fingers. We have become a generation of users. We use God for convenience and are critical if He doesn't do things as we see fit. We expect God to serve us, not we serve God.

The Scripture tells us to seek Godly counsel but not with a secular origin.
Psalms 1:1-6 NLT: *Oh, the joys of those who do not follow the advice of the wicked, or stand around with sinners, or join in with mockers. But they delight in the law of the LORD, meditating on it day and night. They are like trees planted along the riverbank, bearing fruit each season. Their leaves never wither, and they prosper in all they do. But not the wicked! They are like worthless chaff, scattered by the wind. They will be condemned at the time of judgment. Sinners will have no place among the godly. For the LORD watches over the path of the godly, but the path of the wicked leads to destruction.*

2 Peter 1:3-9 NLT: <u>By his divine power, God has given us everything we need for living a godly life. We have received all of this by coming to know him, the one who called us to himself by means of his marvelous glory and excellence. And because of his glory and excellence, he has given us great and precious promises. These are the promises that enable you to share his divine nature and escape the world's corruption caused by human desires. Given all this, make every effort to respond to God's promises. Supplement your faith with a generous provision of moral excellence, and moral excellence with knowledge, and knowledge with self-control, and self-control with patient endurance, and patient endurance with godliness, and godliness with brotherly affection, and brotherly affection with love for everyone. The more you grow like this, the more productive and useful you will be in your knowledge of our Lord Jesus Christ. But those who fail to develop in this way are shortsighted or blind, forgetting that they have been cleansed from their old sins.</u>

WHAT IS SELF-ESTEEM? The American College Dictionary

Self-esteem refers to a favorable opinion of oneself. It can also be associated with the term "conceit," which denotes an exaggerated assessment of one's abilities, importance, or wit, often leading to self-flattery. Related concepts include vanity, egotism, and complacency.

Pride, a term closely linked to self-esteem, is characterized by a high or excessive opinion of one's dignity, importance, merit, or superiority. This perception can manifest either mentally or in one's behavior. Pride, which encompasses feeling proud, plays a significant role in self-esteem, contributing to a dignified sense of what one deserves regarding one's position or character.

<u>Scriptures concerning what God thinks about Pride:</u>

Psalms 10:4 NLT: <u>The wicked are too proud to seek God. They seem to think that God is dead.</u>

Psalms 18:27 NLT: <u>You rescue the humble, but you humiliate the proud.</u>

Psalms 119:21 NLT: <u>You rebuke the arrogant; those who wander from your commands are cursed.</u>

Psalms 138:6 NLT: <u>Though the LORD is great, he cares for the humble, but he keeps his distance from the proud.</u>

Proverbs 6:16-19 NLT: <u>There are six things the LORD hates--no, seven things he detests:</u>
<u>1. Haughty eyes.</u>
<u>2. A lying tongue.</u>
<u>3. Hands that kill the innocent.</u>
<u>4. A heart that plots evil.</u>
<u>5. Feet that race to do wrong.</u>
<u>6. A false witness who pours out lies.</u>
<u>7. A person who sows discord in a family.</u>

Proverbs 8:13 NLT: <u>All who fear the LORD will hate evil. Therefore, I hate Pride and arrogance, corruption and perverse speech.</u>

Proverbs 11:2 NLT: <u>Pride leads to disgrace, but with humility comes wisdom.</u>

Proverbs 13:10 NLT: <u>Pride leads to conflict; those who take advice are wise.</u>

Proverbs 15:32-33 NLT: <u>If you reject discipline, you only harm yourself; but if you listen to correction, you grow in understanding. Fear of the LORD teaches wisdom; humility precedes honor.</u>

Proverbs 16:5 NLT: <u>The LORD detests the proud; they will surely be punished.</u>

Proverbs 16:18-19 NLT: <u>Pride goes before destruction, and haughtiness before a fall. Better to live humbly with the poor than to share plunder with the proud.</u>

Pride is difficult to deal with. It refuses to take responsibility, humble itself, and pray when convicted of wrongdoing. Pride says, "MY WILL," not "YOURS, LORD!"

Through psychology, Pride is now an acceptable attribute. The word for Pride may have changed to self-esteem, but the origin is still the same.

COSMETICS
"ENCYCLOPEDIA AMERICANA" 1995
COSMETICS: (From the Greek kosmetikos, meaning "skilled in adornment") are as old as humanity. The earliest forms of cosmetics applied to the skin by primitive peoples were derived from simple vegetable colorings–herbs, roots, berries, and nuts." [16]

Cosmetics was initially located under the topic "Masks."

"MAN, MYTH & MAGIC" An Illustrated Encyclopedia of Mythology, Religion and the Unknown"

MASKS MEANS A CHANGE OF IDENTITY: "Put on a mask, and you become a different person. In many primitive societies, a mask is more than a means of changing your appearance; it is a link with the world of the spirits, a channel by which men can tap the force possessed by supernatural beings." [17]

HIDDEN IDENTITY: "In primitive societies today, masks are used mainly for ritual purposes. The donning of a mask is believed to change a man's identity and faculties, for the assumed appearance is held to affect the wearer's inner nature and to assimilate it to that of the being represented by the mask. Thus, a masked person is not simply a man or woman whose real identity is hidden. Still, he is an enigmatic entity standing outside the sphere of ordinary conduct and enjoying a freedom of movement and expression denied to ordinary men. As he has submerged his identity by wearing a mask, other beings, such as an ancestor, a spirit, or a totem - -animal, can manifest themselves in his body and voice." [18]

"Of a different order are the masks of shamans - priests and spirit - media - who establish contact between man and the world of supernatural beings (see SHAMAN). The shamans of the Eskimo have masks representing their GUARDIAN SPIRITS, and they believe that by wearing these masks, they establish a mystic link with the spirit concerned and induce a state of trance and possession." [19]

"Where the mask has lost its religious significance, it can still survive in a secular role. Typical of this development was its role in the theater of ancient Greece (see Drama). Originally, animal masks had been used in the Dionysus and Demeter, the Earth Mother cult. Later, the mask found its way into the comedies and the tragedies of the classical theater, where it played an important role. The masks enabled actors to double and triple the number of parts they could play during any performance, and male actors could convincingly play female roles." [20]

PURPOSE BEHIND THE MASKS: "Protection against supernatural dangers is a function of masks worn in certain ritual situations, such as at funerals, to avoid recognition by the souls of the dead. Conversely, masks are sometimes worn to enhance a warrior's image and to terrify opponents, and this idea underlies the war masks and use of war paint among many primitive peoples. The warrior wearing a mask symbolizes a superior power, identifies himself with this force, and is thereby being fortified in spirit. This identification is part of the nature of masks, and it assumes enormous importance where people wear masks representing gods and other supernatural beings." [21]

"The masks of such societies also concentrate power in the hands of those in charge of the sacred objects. Thus, they are linked not only with the representation of power but also with its exercise. The human guardian and wearer of the mask partake of the power of the divinity or spirit that the mask symbolizes and is elevated above the uninitiated's common mass. The mask is thus a link with the supernatural world and a channel by which men can tap the force possessed by supernatural beings. Thus, masks are and always were primary means of transformation and identification with the entities of a non-material sphere to which man has access only if he sheds his own identity and enters that of beings existing on a superior plane." [22]

Performers initially used masks, and over time, modifications were made to make application easier. Artists found that painting the face could create better visual representations. Actors and actresses began to wear Makeup off-stage, and the public adopted the look.

"THE SECRET LIFE OF COSMETICS" A Science Experiment Book by Vicki Cobb 1985 {this book was found in the children's section of the library}

MAKEUP
"Makeup is a fashion that changes with the times. People worldwide have decorated their faces and bodies with paint from ancient times to the present. The first face and body painters were not so interested in being beautiful as in pleasing the gods. But Cleopatra, the beautiful queen of Ancient Egypt who lived about 2,000 years ago, may have been the first to set a trend in eye makeup. Cleopatra painted her eyes with kohl, a black, green, or blue powder containing "antimony ." Antimony compounds may be colored and are used as pigments. Cleopatra put black kohl on her upper eyelids and more kohl on her eyelashes. She painted the areas just under her eyes green or blue. Poppaea, the beautiful wife of Nero, the cruel Roman emperor who ruled almost 2,000 years ago, painted her face white with a mixture of white lead and grease. Cleopatra and Poppaea were among the first of a long line of royal women who set their day's standards for beauty and fashion." [23]

SIGNS IN THE NAILS
"The practice of decorating the fingers has been carried out for medical and magical purposes in the past." [24]

"The ancient Egyptians practiced the decoration of fingernails to ward off evil spirits. It was one of the minor idolatries banned in Cromwell's England. Chinese mandarins gilded their fingernails as a sign of rank, and men and women of mixed blood in Spain and America used to color them to conceal their ancestry, which their nails would otherwise betray." [25]

Leviticus 19:28-34 NLT: "Do not cut your bodies for the dead, and do not mark your skin with tattoos. I am the LORD. "Do not defile your daughter by making her a prostitute, or the land will be filled with prostitution and wickedness. "Keep my Sabbath days of rest, and show reverence toward my sanctuary. I am the LORD. "Do not defile yourselves by turning to mediums or to those who consult the spirits of the dead. I am the LORD your God. "Stand up in the presence of the elderly, and show respect for the aged. Fear your God. I am the LORD. "Do not take advantage of foreigners who live among you in your land. Treat them like native-born Israelites, and love them as you love yourself. Remember that you were once foreigners living in the land of Egypt. I am the LORD your God.

The connection between tattooing and the occult is complex and rooted in ancient practices and symbolism. While tattoos are often seen as a form of self-expression and body art, some designs and practices have been associated with occult beliefs and rituals.

Here are some of how tattooing has been linked to the occult:
Ancient Origins:
- **Shamanic Traditions:** In many ancient cultures, tattooing was a sacred practice performed by shamans. Tattoos were believed to have spiritual significance, offering protection, enhancing power, and connecting individuals to the spirit world.
- **Symbolism:** Many ancient tattoo designs, such as those in Polynesian and Egyptian cultures, were imbued with symbolic meaning. These symbols often represented deities, spirits, or protective forces.

Modern Interpretations:
- **Occult Symbolism:** Some tattoo designs incorporate symbols associated with the occult, such as pentagrams, inverted crosses, and sigils. These symbols may be chosen for their aesthetic appeal or perceived spiritual or magical properties.
- **Spiritual Beliefs:** For some individuals, tattoos can serve as a personal expression of their spiritual beliefs or practices. They may choose designs representing their connection to a higher power or a specific spiritual path.
- **Ritualistic Practices:** In certain occult traditions, tattooing may be seen as a ceremonial act. Getting a tattoo can be viewed as a form of initiation or transformation, marking a significant change in an individual's life.

It's important to note that not all tattoos with occult symbolism are necessarily connected to harmful practices. However, it's crucial to be aware of the potential associations and to choose designs that resonate with evil spirits.

Tattooing, along with body piercing, is forbidden according to the Word of God. They were banned because they represented occultic pagan practices.

"MAN, MYTH & MAGIC" An Illustrated Encyclopedia of Mythology, Religion and the Unknown"

THE URGE TO ENHANCE the beauty of the human body by artificial means is worldwide, but the techniques of doing so differ from culture to culture and age to age. Among people who do not wear clothes or whose clothing is sparse, efforts at altering the body's natural appearance concentrate on decorating the actual surface of the skin. The most prevalent methods of achieving this may be painting, tattooing, and cicatrization.

Painting includes all types of decoration in which colored substances are applied to the skin without causing permanent discoloration. Tattooing consists of pricking pigment into the skin to produce a permanent pattern, usually black or blue, under a smooth surface. [26]

"Cicatrization, which involves the artificial creation of scars, is effected by scratching, cutting, piercing or burning the skin. The wounds may be allowed to heal naturally, forming plain scars that are usually slightly depressed or aggravated to form deep gashes. Raised scars may be produced by continued and extremely painful irritation, which results in the proliferation of regenerative tissue." [27]

The Egyptians used tattooing to honor the names of their pagan deities and display their occultic symbols.

As we have seen so far, the use of cosmetics varies in one form or another.

Cosmetics have become a multibillion-dollar industry.

Going to the supermarket can undoubtedly be a trip of total depression, as we are reminded about our appearance. Numerous magazines display articles such as How to Dress for Success, Proper Application of Cosmetics, Weight Control and How to Lose 10 Pounds in Two Weeks, The Ten Best Dressed and The Ten Worse Dressed Women of the Year, How to Marry the Man of Your Dreams, etc. Or, watch television to be shown your physical inadequacies.

No wonder people visit psychologists to feel better about themselves.

The New Age Movement extensively promotes the idea that we are gods within ourselves. Women are told to enhance their beauty to become the goddesses they were intended to be. Satanism, on the other hand, dictates to women that to be a **"TRUE SATANIC WITCH,"** they need to wear light Makeup, trim their hair, and add a little jewelry.

Considering all the facts, there is just too much at stake, both naturally and spiritually, to allow Satan one foothold.

Chapter 8
Trojan Horse

The Trojan War is a legendary conflict in Greek mythology that took place around the 12th or 13th century BC. The Achaeans (Greeks) waged it against the city of Troy after Paris of Troy took Helen from her husband Menelaus, king of Sparta.

Key Points of the Trojan War:
- **The Abduction of Helen:** The Trojan prince Paris's abduction of Helen, Menelaus's beautiful wife, sparked the war.
- **The Achaean Alliance:** To avenge the abduction, Menelaus and his brother Agamemnon, the king of Mycenae, assembled a large army of Greek warriors, including legendary heroes like Achilles, Odysseus, and Ajax.
- **The Siege of Troy:** The Achaeans laid siege to Troy for ten years. The city's strong fortifications and the bravery of its defenders made it difficult to conquer.
- **The Trojan Horse:** The Achaeans devised a cunning plan: they built a giant wooden horse and hid soldiers inside. The Trojans, believing it to be a gift, brought the horse into their city. At night, the soldiers emerged and opened the gates to the Achaean army.
- **The Fall of Troy:** With the city's defenses breached, the Achaeans sacked Troy, destroying it and killing many inhabitants.

The Trojan War is one of the most important events in Greek mythology and has been the subject of numerous works of literature, art, and film. Homer's epic poems, the Iliad and the Odyssey, are the most famous accounts of the war.

In the narrative, a strategic scheme is devised to take control of the city, coinciding with the malicious intentions of dark forces aiming to eradicate humanity.

The Trojan Horse is a legendary device used by the Greeks to infiltrate the city of Troy during the Trojan War. Here's a breakdown of the story:

The Story:
- **The Siege:** After a decade-long siege, the Greeks, frustrated by their inability to conquer the city, devised a cunning plan.
- **The Wooden Horse:** They built a massive wooden horse and hid a select group of soldiers inside.
- **The Deception:** The Greeks pretended to retreat, leaving the horse as a gift to the gods.
- **The Trojan Mistake:** Despite warnings from some, the Trojans believed the horse to be a harmless offering and pulled it into the city.
- **The Attack:** At night, the hidden soldiers emerged from the horse, opened the city gates, and let in the rest of the Greek army.
- **The Fall of Troy:** The Greeks sacked the city, ending the long and arduous war.

Symbolism of the Trojan Horse: The Trojan Horse is a powerful metaphor illustrating the concept of deceptive strategies. It symbolizes scenarios where something may appear harmless on the surface but conceals a hidden threat. This metaphor applies to various tactics that utilize disguise to gain entry or trust.

Legacy of the Trojan Horse: The story of the Trojan Horse has endured through the ages, inspiring many literary, artistic, and cinematic works. It underscores the notion of deception and emphasizes the necessity for vigilance, particularly in situations involving seemingly innocuous gifts or offers.

Contemporary Interpretation: In 2024, the Trojan Horse can be likened to the modern cell phone. While these devices provide numerous conveniences and benefits, they also have potential risks and dangers that warrant caution.

Here are some key concerns:

Health Risks:

- **Radiation Exposure:** Cell phones emit radiofrequency (RF) radiation, which is non-ionizing. While current research hasn't definitively linked RF radiation to serious health problems like cancer, some studies suggest potential risks, especially for long-term and heavy users.
- **Brain Tumors:** There have been concerns about a possible link between cell phone use and certain types of brain tumors, particularly acoustic neuromas and gliomas.

However, the evidence needs to be more conclusive, and more research is required.

- **Sleep Disruptions:** The blue light emitted by cell phone screens can interfere with sleep patterns, potentially leading to insomnia, fatigue, and other health issues.
- **Neck and Back Pain:** Prolonged use of cell phones can lead to poor posture and strain the neck and back muscles.
- **Eye Strain:** Staring at screens for extended periods can cause eye strain, headaches, and dry eyes.

Safety Hazards:

- **Distracted Driving:** Using cell phones while driving increases the risk of accidents.
- **Cyberbullying and Online Harassment:** Cell phones can be used to engage in cyberbullying and online harassment, causing emotional distress and harm.
- **Addiction:** Excessive use of cell phones can lead to addiction, negatively impacting mental health and relationships.
- **Privacy Concerns:** Cell phones collect much personal data, raising concerns about privacy and security breaches.

Tips for Safe Cell Phone Use:

- **Limit Screen Time:** Reduce time spent on cell phones, especially before bed.
- **Use Headsets:** Minimize direct exposure to RF radiation using headsets or speakerphones.
- **Practice Good Posture:** Avoid hunching over your phone and take frequent breaks.
- **Be Mindful of Distractions:** Put your phone away while driving, crossing the street, or in social situations.
- **Protect Your Privacy:** Be cautious about sharing personal information online and use strong passwords.

Remember, moderation is key. By being aware of the potential dangers and taking steps to minimize risks, you can enjoy the benefits of cell phones while protecting your health and well-being.

Cell phones have undoubtedly revolutionized communication and information access, but they also come with social dangers that can negatively impact individuals and society. Here are some of the critical social risks associated with cell phone use:

Addiction and Mental Health:
• **Screen Addiction:** Excessive use of cell phones can lead to addiction, characterized by compulsive checking, anxiety when away from the device, and difficulty focusing on other tasks.
• **Mental Health Issues:** Screen addiction has been linked to increased rates of depression, anxiety, and loneliness.
• **Sleep Disruptions:** The blue light emitted by cell phone screens can interfere with sleep patterns, leading to insomnia and other sleep-related problems.

Social Isolation and Reduced Real-World Interactions:
• **Decreased Face-to-Face Communication:** Constant phone use can reduce face-to-face interactions, hindering the development of social skills and emotional intelligence.
• **Isolation and Loneliness:** Overreliance on online communication can lead to feelings of isolation and loneliness, particularly among young people.

Cyberbullying and Online Harassment:
• **Harmful Content:** Cell phones can be used to spread harmful content, including cyberbullying, hate speech, and online harassment.
• **Emotional Distress:** Exposure to such content can cause significant emotional distress and mental health problems.

Distracted Driving and Safety Hazards:
• **Accidents:** Using cell phones while driving is a significant cause of accidents, resulting in injuries and fatalities.
• **Reduced Attention:** Phone use can distract individuals from their surroundings, increasing the risk of accidents and other safety hazards.

Privacy Concerns and Data Breaches:
- **Personal Data:** Cell phones collect vast amounts of personal data, raising concerns about privacy and security.
- **Data Breaches:** Data breaches can expose sensitive information, leading to identity theft and other forms of fraud.

Financial Implications:
- **Overspending:** Cell phone plans and app purchases can lead to significant financial burdens, especially for young people and those with limited budgets.

Given the social dangers associated with excessive cell phone use, engaging in mindful technology practices is essential. This can be achieved by consciously setting limits on screen time and ensuring that we dedicate sufficient time to face-to-face interactions with friends and family. By prioritizing real-world connections, we can nurture social skills and strengthen relationships.

Additionally, it is crucial to remain aware of the potential downsides of spending too much time on our devices. This can lead to feelings of isolation and hinder our ability to engage fully with the world around us. These strategies can create a healthier balance between our digital lives and meaningful personal interactions.

Cell phones can have a significant negative impact on relationships, primarily due to the following factors:

1. Distraction and Lack of Presence:
- **Reduced Attention:** Constant phone use during conversations or shared activities can make individuals feel unimportant and undervalued.
- **Missed Opportunities:** Distractions from phones can lead to missed opportunities for meaningful connection and bonding.

2. Miscommunication and Conflict:
- **Misinterpretation:** Text messages and social media posts can be misinterpreted, leading to misunderstandings and arguments.
- **Lack of Nuance:** Written communication lacks the nuances of tone and body language, which can be crucial for effective communication.

3. Privacy and Trust Issues:

- **Oversharing:** Excessive sharing of personal information online can lead to privacy concerns and erode trust within relationships.
- **Jealousy and Insecurity:** Constant phone use can fuel jealousy and insecurity, particularly when partners are perceived as spending more time on their devices than with their loved ones.

4. Social Isolation and Loneliness:

- **Reduced Face-to-Face Interaction:** Overreliance on online communication can decrease face-to-face interaction, hindering the development of strong social bonds.
- **Isolation:** Spending more time on phones can lead to isolation and loneliness, even when surrounded by people.

5. Addiction and Compulsive Behavior:

- **Screen Addiction:** Excessive phone use can lead to addiction, making it challenging to prioritize relationships and other essential aspects of life.
- **Negative Impact on Mental Health:** Screen addiction has been linked to increased rates of depression, anxiety, and other mental health issues.

To mitigate these adverse effects, practice mindful phone use, set boundaries, and prioritize quality time with loved ones. Awareness of phone habits and consciously connecting with others can strengthen our relationships and improve our overall well-being.

The things that I am pointing out in this chapter are apparent. Families suffer from a lack of interaction.

Social media refers to interactive computer-mediated technologies that facilitate the creation and sharing of information, ideas, career interests, and other forms of expression via virtual communities and networks. It encompasses many internet-based applications, such as social networking sites, blogs, microblogging platforms, and social bookmarking sites.

The Dark Side of Video Recording: Cruelty and Exploitation

While video recording technology has brought many benefits, it has also been used to facilitate and perpetuate cruelty and exploitation. Here are some of the negative aspects:

Cyberbullying and Harassment:
- **Public Humiliation:** Videos can be used to humiliate individuals, spreading them widely online publicly.
- **Threats and Intimidation:** Videos can be used to threaten and intimidate victims, leading to severe emotional distress.

Revenge Porn:
- **Non-Consensual Sharing:** Private, intimate videos can be shared without consent, causing significant emotional harm and reputational damage.

Animal Cruelty:
- **Graphic Content:** Videos depicting animal cruelty can be disturbing and harmful to animals and viewers.
- **Online Market:** Unfortunately, there is a market for such videos, fueling the demand for animal abuse.

Exploitation of Vulnerable Individuals:
- **Child Exploitation:** Children can be exploited for the production of child sexual abuse material.
- **Elder Abuse:** Vulnerable adults can be targeted and abused, with their experiences captured on video.

Distracted Driving and Accidents:
- **Recording While Driving:** Recording videos can distract drivers, leading to accidents and endangering lives.

Privacy Violations:
- **Secret Recording:** People may be secretly recorded in public or private spaces without their consent, violating their privacy.

It's essential to use video recording technology responsibly and ethically. By being aware of the potential negative consequences, we can help prevent the misuse of this powerful tool.

Deepfakes can be used for various purposes, both harmless and harmful. Some examples include:

- **Entertainment:** Creating humorous or creative content, such as celebrity lip-syncs or fictional scenarios.
- **Education:** Simulating historical events or demonstrating complex concepts.

- **Misinformation and Disinformation:** Spreading false information or propaganda, manipulating public opinion, or damaging reputations.
- **Fraud:** Impersonating individuals for financial gain or other malicious purposes.

As deepfake technology becomes more sophisticated, it's essential to be aware of its potential impact and critically evaluate online content's authenticity. This technology creates a strong deception.

Deception is misleading someone by presenting false information or concealing the truth. It involves intentionally creating a false impression to gain an advantage or avoid negative consequences.

Forms of Deception:
- **Lies:** Making false statements with the intent to deceive.
- **Omissions:** Withholding relevant information would significantly alter the other person's understanding.
- **Misrepresentations:** Distorting the truth or presenting it misleadingly.
- **Manipulation:** Using psychological tactics to influence someone's thoughts or actions without full awareness.

Reasons for Deception:
- **Self-protection:** Avoiding punishment or negative consequences.
- **Self-gain:** Obtaining personal benefits, such as money, power, or approval.
- **Self-preservation:** Maintaining one's reputation or social standing.
- **Self-deception:** Believing one's false narratives or justifications.

Ethical Considerations:
Deception can have profound ethical implications, as it undermines trust and honesty. It can damage relationships, harm reputations, and lead to legal consequences. While deception may sometimes be used for seemingly justifiable reasons, it is crucial to consider the potential harm and long-term consequences before engaging in such behavior.

Pranking is playing a trick on someone, often intended to be humorous or surprising. It involves a playful deception or surprise, usually causing amusement or confusion.

Pranks can range from simple, harmless jokes to more elaborate schemes. Some common examples include:

- **Classic Pranks:** A classic prank replaces toothpaste with a similar-looking substance, such as mayonnaise or shaving cream.
- Putting a whoopee cushion on someone's chair.
- When playing a practical joke using a rubber snake or spider.
- **Modern Pranks:** Using technology to create elaborate pranks, such as hacking into social media accounts or sending fake messages.
- It creates elaborate video pranks that go viral on platforms like YouTube.

While pranks can be considered harmless fun, they can also have negative consequences. Here are some of the dangers associated with pranks:

Physical Harm:

- **Accidents:** Pranks involving physical activity or objects can lead to accidents, such as slips, falls, or injuries.
- **Property Damage:** Pranks that involve damaging property, such as throwing objects or tampering with belongings, can result in costly repairs.

Emotional Harm:

- **Hurt Feelings:** Hurtful or embarrassing Pranks can damage relationships and cause emotional distress.
- **Anxiety and Fear:** Pranks that involve unexpected scares or threats can cause stress and fear, especially in vulnerable individuals.

Legal Consequences:

- **Criminal Charges:** In some cases, pranks can lead to criminal charges, such as vandalism, assault, or harassment.
- **Civil Lawsuits:** Victims of pranks may sue for damages, including medical expenses and emotional distress.

Social Consequences:

- **Damaged Reputation:** Pranks that go too far can damage a person's reputation and lead to social isolation.
- **Loss of Trust:** Pranks can erode trust between individuals and groups.

It is essential to evaluate the possible consequences before proceeding with a prank. While some pranks may seem harmless, they can quickly escalate into dangerous or hurtful situations. If there's any doubt about the appropriateness of a prank, it is advisable to forgo it entirely.

Refrain from making others the target of jokes, as this behavior can be considered unkind and cruel.

The term **'provoke'** can be a double-edged sword. It can mean stimulating or inciting a specific reaction or feeling in someone, which can be positive or negative depending on the context.

Positive Connotations:
- **Stimulate Thought:** Provoking can mean encouraging deep thought or discussion.
- **Inspire Action:** It can also mean motivating someone to take action or make a change.

Negative Connotations:
- **Anger or Aggression:** Provoking can mean deliberately trying to make someone angry or upset, often to start a fight or argument.
- **Negative Emotions:** It can also mean causing negative emotions like fear, anxiety, or jealousy.

The term "provoke" carries different meanings based on the context and the intent of the action involved. In biblical teachings, there is a general warning against provoking others, particularly in a way that incites anger. Several key verses highlight this principle, underscoring the importance of considering the implications of our actions on others' emotions and responses.

Ephesians 6:4: "Fathers, do not provoke your children to anger, but bring them up in the discipline and instruction of the Lord."

Proverbs 19:11: "The discretion of a man delays his anger, and it is glory for him to overlook transgression."

Romans 12:19: "Beloved, never avenge yourselves, but leave it to the wrath of God, for it is written, "Vengeance is mine, I will repay," says the Lord."

These verses suggest that provoking others can lead to negative consequences, such as anger, resentment, and violence. Instead, the Bible encourages us to be patient, kind, and forgiving.

However, there are instances in the Bible where God provoked people to act in certain ways, often for a specific purpose. For example, God provoked Pharaoh to harden his heart so that He could demonstrate His power through the plagues.

It's important to note that these instances are specific to the divine plan and should not be taken as a justification for provoking others in everyday life.

DEUTERONOMY 32:21 NLT: *They have roused my jealousy by worshiping things that are not God; they have provoked my anger with their useless idols. Now I will rouse their jealousy through people who are not even a people; I will provoke their anger through the foolish Gentiles.*

1 Kings 16:33 NLT: *Then he set up an Asherah pole. He did more to provoke the anger of the LORD, the God of Israel, than any of the other kings of Israel before him.*

2 Kings 23:26 NLT: *Even so, the LORD was very angry with Judah because of all the wicked things Manasseh had done to provoke him.*

Job 12:6 NLT: *But robbers are left in peace, and those who provoke God live in safety--though God keeps them in his power.*

Isaiah 3:8 NLT: *stumble, and Judah will fall, because they speak out against the LORD and refuse to obey him. They provoke him to his face.*

Jeremiah 25:6 NLT: *Do not provoke my anger by worshiping idols you made with your own hands. Then I will not harm you.'*

Jeremiah 44:8 NLT: <u>Why provoke my anger by burning incense to the idols you have made here in Egypt? You will only destroy yourselves and make yourselves an object of cursing and mockery for all the nations of the earth.</u>

Galatians 5:26 NLT: <u>Let us not become conceited, or provoke one another, or be jealous of one another.</u>

Ephesians 6:4 NLT: <u>Fathers, do not provoke your children to anger by the way you treat them. Rather, bring them up with the discipline and instruction that comes from the Lord.</u>

In closing, you must have the right attitude and reflect the attributes of God. Galatians 5:22-23 NLT: But the Holy Spirit produces this kind of fruit in our lives: love, joy, peace, patience, kindness, goodness, faithfulness, gentleness, and self-control. There is no law against these things!

PDF AVAILABLE WITH DONATION AT THE FOLLOWING EMAIL: atlife@yahoo.com

Endnotes

Caught Unaware

1. Gods, Pagan, Nelson's Illustrated Bible Dictionary, (Thomas Nelson Publishers, 1986)

2. Gods, Pagan, Nelson's Illustrated Bible Dictionary, (Thomas Nelson Publishers, 1986)

3. Gods, Pagan, Nelson's Illustrated Bible Dictionary, (Thomas Nelson Publishers, 1986)

4. Gods, Pagan, Nelson's Illustrated Bible Dictionary, (Thomas Nelson Publishers, 1986)

5. Gods, Pagan, Nelson's Illustrated Bible Dictionary, (Thomas Nelson Publishers, 1986)

6. Gods, Pagan, Nelson's Illustrated Bible Dictionary, (Thomas Nelson Publishers, 1986)

7. Gods, Pagan, Nelson's Illustrated Bible Dictionary, (Thomas Nelson Publishers, 1986)

8. Gods, Pagan, Nelson's Illustrated Bible Dictionary, (Thomas Nelson Publishers, 1986)

9. Gods, Pagan, Nelson's Illustrated Bible Dictionary, (Thomas Nelson Publishers, 1986)

10. Gods, Pagan, Nelson's Illustrated Bible Dictionary, (Thomas Nelson Publishers, 1986)

11. Gods, Pagan, Nelson's Illustrated Bible Dictionary, (Thomas Nelson Publishers, 1986)

12. Gods, Pagan, Nelson's Illustrated Bible Dictionary, (Thomas Nelson Publishers, 1986)

13. Gods, Pagan, Nelson's Illustrated Bible Dictionary, (Thomas Nelson Publishers, 1986)

14. Gods, Pagan, Nelson's Illustrated Bible Dictionary, (Thomas Nelson Publishers, 1986)

15. Gods, Pagan, Nelson's Illustrated Bible Dictionary, (Thomas Nelson Publishers, 1986)

16. Gods, Pagan, Nelson's Illustrated Bible Dictionary, (Thomas Nelson Publishers, 1986)

17. Gods, Pagan, Nelson's Illustrated Bible Dictionary, (Thomas Nelson Publishers, 1986)

18. Ficker, Amulet, The New Schaff-Herzog Encyclopedia of Religious Knowledge, Vol 1. (Grand Rapids, MI: Baker Book House, 1967) p. 159.

19. ibid., p. 159, 160.

20. ibid., p. 160.

21. ibid., p. 160.

22. ibid., p. 160.

23. ibid., p. 160.

24. Benzinger, Dress and Ornament, Hebrew, The New Schaff-Herzog Encyclopedia of Religious Knowledge, Vol 4. (Grand Rapids, MI: Baker Book House, 1967) p. 5.

25. Ross, Heather Colyer, The Art of Bedouin Jewellry: A Saudi Arabian Profile, (Studio City, CA: EPS/Players Press, 1994) p. 58.

26. Guiley, Rosemary Ellen, Encyclopedia of Witches and Witchcraft, (New York: Facts on File, 1989) p. 335.

27. ibid., p. 9.

28. ibid.

29. ibid., p. 10.

30. ibid.

31. P.M.B., Jewelry, Encyclopedia Britannica, Vol. 12. (Chicago: William Benton, Publisher, 1970) p. 1030.

32. ibid.

33. ibid.

34. ibid.

35. Israel, New Encyclopedia Britannica, Vol. 22. (Chicago: Encyclopedia Britannica, 1992) p. 137.

36. ibid.

37. Liungman, Dictionary of Symbols, (Santa Barbara, CA: ABC-CLIO, 1991) p. 272.

38. ibid.

39. ibid., p. 273.

40. ibid., p. 5.

41. ibid., p. 10.

42. ibid., p. 117.

43. ibid.

44. ibid., p. 188.

45. ibid., p. 259.

46. ibid.

47. ibid., p. 291.

48. ibid., p. 357, 358.

49. ibid., p. 63, 64.

50. ibid., p. 283.

51. ibid., p. 284.

52. Matlins, Antoinette Leonard, Engagement and Wedding Rings, (New York: Gemstone Press, 1990) p. 5.

53. ibid., p. 6.

54. ibid., p. 6.

55. ibid., p. 6.

56. ibid., p. 6, 7.

57. ibid., p. 8.

58. ibid., p. 9.

59. ibid., p. 10.

60. ibid., p. 12.

61. ibid., p. 15.

62. Liungman, Dictionary of Symbols, (Santa Barbara, CA: ABC-CLIO, 1991) p. 154, 155.

63. ibid., p. 185.

64. ibid., p. 203.

65. ibid., p. 308.

66. Melton, Introductory Essay: An Overview of the New Age Movement, The New Age Encyclopedia, First Ed. (Detroit, MI: Gale Research Inc., 1990) p. xiv.

67. ibid., p. xxiii.

68. ibid., p. xxvi.

69. Ankerberg, Facts on Holistic Health and the New Medicine, (Eugene, OR: Harvest House Publishers, 1992) p. 22, 23.

70. Ankerberg, Facts on the New Age Movement, (Eugene, OR: Harvest House Publishers, 1988) p. 18.

71. ibid.

What God Hates

1. Laver, Modesty in Dress; an inquiry into the fundamentals of fashion, (Boston: Houghton Mifflin Co., 1969) p. 28.

2. Weatherford, American Women's History, (New York: Prentice - Hall Inc., 1994) p.196. paraphrased.

3. ibid., p. 42. paraphrased.

4. ibid., p. 42.

5. ibid., p. 42.

6. ibid., p. 42.

7. ibid., p. 320.

8. Oakley, Elizabeth Cady Stanton, (Old Westbury, New York: Feminist Press, 1972) p. 20.

9. ibid., p. 20

10. ibid., p. 34.

11. ibid. p. 322.

12. ibid. p. 322.

13. ibid. p. 322.

14. Oakley, Elizabeth Cady Stanton, (Old Westbury, New York: Feminist Press, 1972) p. 129.

15. ibid., p. 130.

16. Riegel, American Feminists, (Lawrence, Kansas: University of Kansas Press, 1963) p. 61.

17. Oakley, Elizabeth Cady Stanton, (Old Westbury, New York: Feminist Press, 1972) p.130.

18. Weatherford, American Women's History, (New York: Prentice - Hall Inc., 1994) p. 322

19. Hall, From Hoopskirts to Nudity, (Caldwell, ID: The Caxton printers, Ltd., 1938) p. 215, 216.

20. Weatherford, American Women's History, (New York: Prentice - Hall Inc., 1994) p. 386, 387.

21. ibid., p. 132, 133.

22. ibid., p. 388.

23. Weatherford, American Women and World War II, (Oxford, NY: Facts on File, Inc. 1990) p.145.

24. O'Hara, Georgina, The Encyclopaedia of Fashion, (New York: Abrams, Inc., 1986) p.117.

25. ibid., p. 142.

26. ibid. p. 187.

27. p. 29. ibid. p. 187.

28. p. 29. ibid. p. 187.

29. ibid., p. 250.

30. Marrs, Mystery Mark of the New Age, (Westchester, IL: Crossway Books, a division of Good News Publishers, 1988) p. 23.

Games People Play

1. Kempner, Television Encyclopedia, (New York: Fairchild Publishing Co., 1948) p. 30.

2. LaVey, The Devil's Notebook, (Portland, OR: Feral House, 1992) p. 84.

3. ibid., p. 84, 85.

4. ibid., p. 86.

5. ibid., p. 86.

6. ibid., p. 87.

7. ibid., p. 88.

8. Phillips, Saturday Morning Mind Control, (Nashville, TN: Oliver-Nelson Books, 1991) p. 10.

9. ibid., p. 15.

10. ibid., p. 34.

11. ibid., p. 35.

12. ibid., p. 41.

13. ibid., p. 42.

14. ibid., p. 50.

15. ibid., p. 110.

16. ibid., p. 110.

17. ibid., p. 110.

18. ibid., p. 110.

19. ibid., p. 110, 111.

20. ibid., p. 111.

21. ibid., p. 111.

22. ibid., p. 111.

23. ibid., p. 111, 112. paraphrased.

24. ibid., p. 115.

25. ibid., p. 112.

26. ibid., p. 114.

27. ibid., p. 118.

28. ibid., p. 118.

Trendsetters

1. Corinthians, New Encyclopedia Britannica, Vol. 3. (Chicago: Britannica, 1992) p. 631.

2. Corinthians, New Encyclopedia Britannica, Vol. 3. (Chicago: Britannica, 1992) p. 631.

3. Corinthians, New Encyclopedia Britannica, Vol. 3. (Chicago: Britannica, 1992) p. 631.

4. Corinthians, New Encyclopedia Britannica, Vol. 3. (Chicago: Britannica, 1992) p. 631.

5. Greece, Ancient, World Book Encyclopedia, Vol. 8. (Chicago: World Book Inc., 1994) p. 367.

6. ibid., p. 979.

7. Erim, Aphrodisias Awakened City of Ancient Art, National Geographic Vol. 141, NO. 6, June 1972. (Washington, DC: National Geographic Society, 1972) p. 774.

8. Benzinger, Hair, and Beard of the Hebrews, The New Schaff-Herzog Encyclopedia of Religious Knowledge, Vol. 5. (Grand Rapids, MI: Baker Book House, 1967) p. 118.

9. Weatherford, American Women's History, (NY: Prentice - Hall Inc., 1994) p. 47.

10. ibid., p. 47, p. 48.

11. ibid., p.132.

Social Media

1. Melton, Introductory Essay: An Overview of the New Age Movement, The New Age Encyclopedia, First Ed. (Detroit, MI: Gale Research Inc., 1990) p. xxvii.

2. Ankerberg, Weldon, The Facts on Self-Esteem, Psychology, and the Recovery Movement, (Eugene, OR: Harvest House Publishers, 1995) p. 8.

3. ibid.

4. ibid., p. 8, 9.

5. ibid., p. 9.

6. ibid., p. 9.

7. ibid., p. 9.

8. ibid., p. 9.

9. ibid., p. 9, 10.

10. ibid., p. 14.

11. ibid., p. 14.

12. ibid., p. 14.

13. ibid., p. 14.

14. ibid., p. 25.

15. Groothuis, Confronting the New Age, (Downers Grove, IL: Intervarsity Press, 1988) p. 175.

16. Sage, Cosmetics, Encyclopedia Americana, 1995, Vol. 8. (Grolier Incorporated, 1995) p. 33.

17. C. Von Furer-Haimendorf, Masks Means To A Change of Identity, Man, Myth & Magic, Vol. 13. (New York: BPC Publishing Ltd., 1970) p. 1756.

18. ibid.

19. ibid., p. 1760.

20. ibid., p. 1764.

21. ibid., p. 1764, 1765.

22. ibid., p. 1765.

23. Cobb, Vicki, The Secret Life Of Cosmetics: A Science Experiment Book, (New York: Harper Collins, 1985) p. 86, 87.

24. Fingers, Signs in the Nails, Man, Myth & Magic, Vol. 7. (New York: BPC Publishing Ltd., 1970) p. 957.

25. ibid.

26. C. Von Furer-Haimendorf, Tattooing, Man, Myth & Magic, Vol. 18. (New York: Marshall Cavendish Corp., 1995) p. 2576.

27. ibid.

www.ingramcontent.com/pod-product-compliance
Lightning Source LLC
Chambersburg PA
CBHW071712090426
42738CB00009B/1754